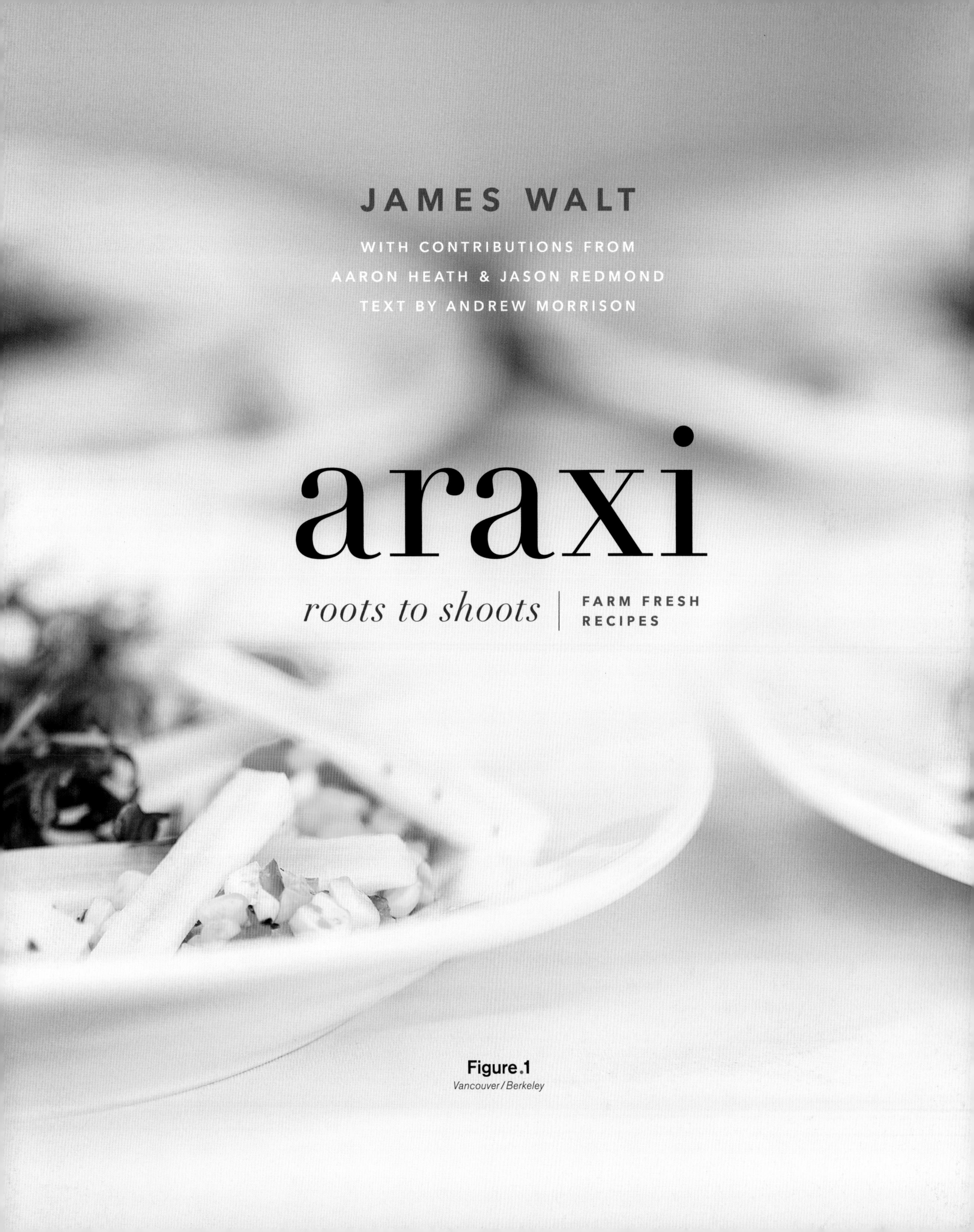

JAMES WALT

WITH CONTRIBUTIONS FROM
AARON HEATH & JASON REDMOND
TEXT BY ANDREW MORRISON

araxi

roots to shoots | FARM FRESH RECIPES

Figure.1
Vancouver / Berkeley

Cataloguing data available from Library and Archives Canada
ISBN 978-1-927958-73-5 (hbk.)

Design and art direction by Jessica Sullivan
Photography by Alison Page and Issha Marie
Inset photo on page 17 by Brandon Hart

Editing by Lucy Kenward
Copy editing by Lesley Cameron
Index by Isabel Steurer

Printed and bound in China by 1010 Printing International, Ltd.
Distributed in the U.S. by Publishers Group West

Figure 1 Publishing Inc.
Vancouver BC Canada
www.figure1pub.com

contents

Introduction 7

Araxi: the highlights 9

Introducing James Walt 12

Araxi's team: the highlights 15

SHOOTS

[MENU 24]

Cocktails 26
Small 30
Larger 56
Desserts 88

LONGTABLE

[MENU 107]

Cocktails 110
Small 112
Larger 120
Desserts 132

ROOTS

[MENU 138]

Cocktails 140
Small 144
Larger 171
Desserts 202

Basics 218

Metric Conversion Table 222

Acknowledgements 224

Index 226

INTRODUCTION

SINCE OPENING DAY in 1981, Araxi Restaurant + Oyster Bar has so thoroughly fused with its address in Whistler's Village Square that it now feels as permanent and immovable as the mountains that loom over it.

Over the years, the restaurant has accepted invitations to bring its uniquely elegant, farm-to-table style of cooking to the James Beard House in New York and ventured far afield to serve stunning, al fresco Longtable Dinners, but it has always returned home to discover that it had never really left. Gordon Ramsay recognized this, famously singling Araxi out as the best restaurant in Canada on account of its total dedication to place. It is why many of the staff can count their tenure there by the decade. It is why this book is in your hands.

Most diners arrive at Araxi by travelling north from Vancouver along a ribbon of road—the Sea-to-Sky Highway—that cuts through some of the most breathtaking scenery on the planet: twisting above Howe Sound's steep, sparkling turquoise fjords; past sparsely inhabited Keats, Anvil and Gambier Islands; beneath the Stawamus Chief's granite monolith and past the broad Squamish River estuary; alongside frigid Alice, Lucille and Daisy Lakes; and close to the thundering mists of Brandywine and Shannon Falls.

After it enters the alpine Whistler Valley—where it is flanked by the glaciated spines of the Garibaldi and Pacific mountain ranges and temperate rainforests of fir, cedar, hemlock and spruce—the road continues north past Araxi's doorstep in Whistler proper, beyond the western shore of Green Lake (fed by the River of Golden Dreams) and down into the Pemberton Valley. That agricultural paradise is dwarfed by jagged, snow-capped Mt. Currie, the slopes of which—in Lil'wat First Nation lore—were scarred by the wriggling of a giant, two-headed serpent and marked by two hunters who were long ago turned to stone.

The land here is so varied in its bounty that—to executive chef James Walt, who calls the valley home—crafting menus from it is more an honour and a privilege than a chore. Many of the farms and ranches that his locally minded kitchen works with directly are located in this valley, like green oases in a white-dune desert of forbidding peaks, shifting glaciers and impenetrable icefields. If you were to continue driving northeast, the road would eventually fork back south and down again into the Okanagan Valley, home to well over 200 wineries, the best of which are well represented in Araxi's legendary cellar, sharing pride of place with the world's top labels.

The restaurant is entirely emblematic of British Columbia. This is not just true in spring, summer and fall when Araxi's sprawling patio spills out into the Village Square. The land and waters that surround it are its playground, larder and school year-round, not only informing all who dine (and work) there of the potential of their own backyard, but also reminding them—deliciously and with inventive intent—of Whistler's founding twin pursuits of pleasure and excellence.

This is more than just a cookbook or a memento of a faraway place once enjoyed; it is a road map back to Araxi's front door and a key to its award-winning kitchen. You are encouraged to use it often.

Toptable's president Michael Doyle (left) with Araxi's executive chef James Walt (right).

ARAXI is the oldest of the award-winning establishments in the Toptable restaurant group, which includes CinCin Ristorante (1990), Blue Water Cafe (2000), West Restaurant (2000), Thierry Cafe (2011) and Bar Oso (2015). When Araxi opened on Halloween night in 1981, there were only four other restaurants in Whistler!

ARAXI is named for the wife of legendary restaurateur and Toptable Group founder Jack Evrensel, who sold Toptable to the Aquilini family in 2014. While upholding the company's well-established standards of excellence and unwavering critical acclaim, the family is firmly committed to ensuring Toptable's evolution and ever-upward trajectory.

MICHAEL DOYLE, Toptable's president, has always worked in hospitality. A dedicated skier, he grew up on Vancouver's mountainous North Shore and made regular pilgrimages to Whistler. When the opportunity arose to be a part of Araxi's dining experience, he says, "It was magical, like a homecoming."

LUIGI AQUILINI has been a farmer for most of his 85 years, growing blueberries and cranberries and raising bees on his farm in Pitt Meadows, BC. His family is also heavily invested in land-based aquaculture, sustainably harvesting both salmon and sablefish.

TIM PICKWELL, who worked in the kitchen at Araxi for exactly 30 years, retired on Halloween in 2011. The restaurant closed early that night, with former colleagues arriving from as far away as the Maritimes to help send him off (in costume, of course).

RESTAURANT DIRECTOR Neil Henderson started skiing in his native Scotland at the age of 7. The only thing that eclipses his love of mountains is his appreciation for food and wine. He began at Araxi as a busser in 1992 and rose through the ranks to lead the restaurant in 1998.

IN 1998, Araxi closed for 6 weeks to morph from a European-themed restaurant to a locally focused one. James Walt, a 28-year-old fresh from 3 years of helming the kitchen at Sooke Harbour House on Vancouver Island, was brought on as executive chef. The renovation cost $500,000.

IN 2013, Araxi launched its now wildly popular Oyster Bar. There are typically up to a dozen oyster varieties on offer, sourced directly from local oyster farms. Over 1,000 are shucked each day at the elegant stainless steel–and-marble bar.

IN 2005, Araxi became a founding member of Ocean Wise, the fledgling Vancouver Aquarium initiative that set out to educate chefs and diners about the importance of choosing sustainable seafood. Today, there are over 600 member restaurants across Canada.

ARAXI has been invited to bring its farm-to-table cooking to the prestigious James Beard House in New York on three occasions (1998, 2002, 2006). James Walt and his team received standing ovations at the conclusion of each sold-out evening.

SINCE 2011, Araxi has hosted special outdoor dinners on impossibly long tables serving hundreds of diners at once. From the first event in the fields at Pemberton's North Arm Farm, the Longtable Dinner series has moved to Lost Lake and Rainbow Parks in Whistler and to Vanier Park in Vancouver.

THE 2009 season of celebrity chef Gordon Ramsay's reality TV show *Hell's Kitchen* saw 16 competitors vying for the opportunity to work at Araxi under Chef Walt. The winner, Dave Levey, toiled through the 2010 Winter Olympics and beyond.

DURING the 2010 Winter Olympics, Araxi never served fewer than 600 people a day for 16 straight days, and was staffed 24 hours a day (deliveries were made between midnight and 4:00 a.m.). Neil Henderson personally organized over 7,000 reservations across all Toptable establishments during that time.

ARAXI'S wine cellar has gone from a 40-bottle shelf worth $400 on opening night to a collection of thousands of bottles worth millions. For oenophiles, Araxi hosts Big Guns, a multi-course feast with wine pairings during Whistler's annual food and wine festival, Cornucopia.

ARAXI wine director Samantha Rahn was named Sommelier of the Year at the Vancouver International Wine Festival in 2013 and was invited to create a wine of her own, the "Samantha" Syrah, at the Crush Pad Winery in BC's Okanagan Valley.

DOZENS of BC's top restaurateurs, bartenders, servers, sommeliers, managers and chefs have honed their skills under Toptable's umbrella. Staff attend weekly training meetings, wine and food tastings, and field trips to artisan suppliers and farms.

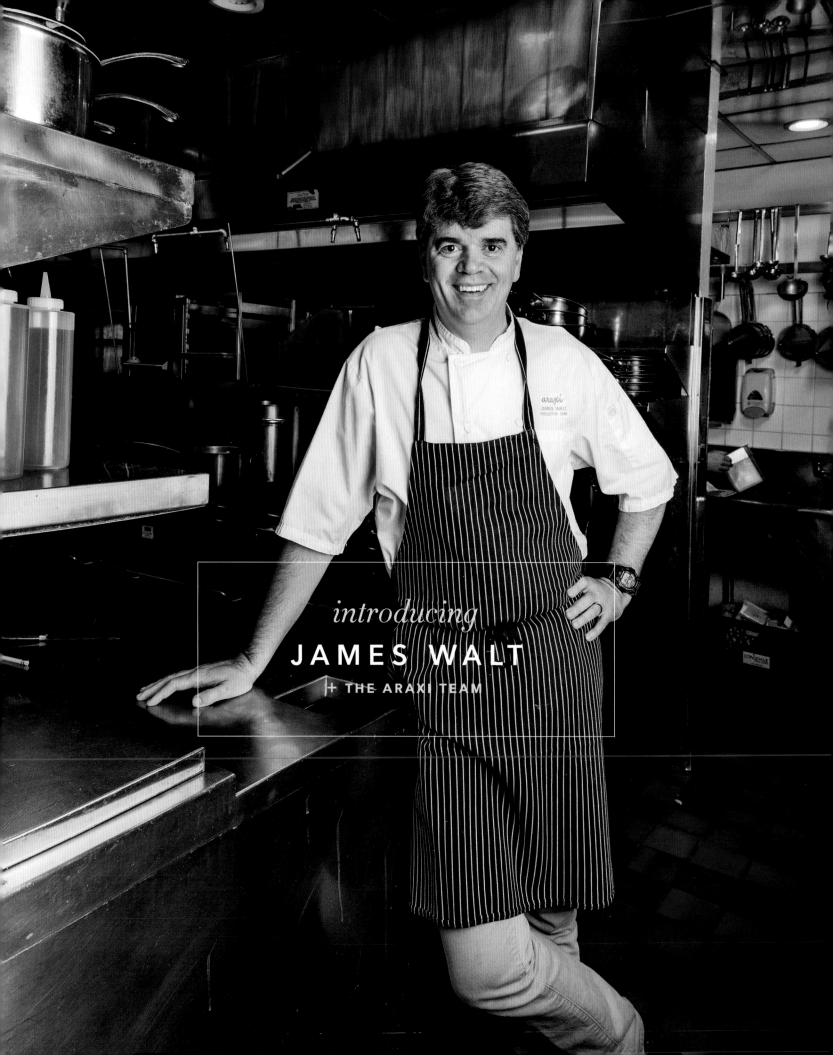

introducing

JAMES WALT

+ THE ARAXI TEAM

LIVING IN an agricultural community in Ontario's Ottawa Valley could be hard going, especially with four sons under the age of 7, but such was the dream of James Walt's father, a military man and civil engineer. He had bought an ancient farmhouse—built before Confederation—located outside of Stittsville. When part of the building collapsed, giving one of the brothers a concussion, the Walts bulldozed what remained and built a new house as a family, all the while growing corn, potatoes, peas, carrots and sometimes even tomatoes.

If that was how James' interest in food was sparked, it may have been the back-breaking work he endured as a member of the farm labour pool that gave the 12-year-old James a deeper understanding of the care and consideration that his mother took with food and the joy she found in preparing food in her kitchen. "My mom went all out on the big family meals," he remembers, and such was her impact that all four of her boys have become the lead cooks in their own households.

Farm life was tough, but James thrived on it. At 13, he was driving a tractor for a vegetable farm outside Kanata as well as washing dishes and doing kitchen prep at a local restaurant. Food, he knew, was his calling, so after high school he packed up for Stratford Chefs School, the best culinary college in Canada.

James and his classmates were seduced by the local-food philosophy of Alice Waters at Berkeley's Chez Panisse and Sinclair Philip at Vancouver Island's Sooke Harbour House, which in the early 1990s had yet to catch on widely. The West Coast called, even though Stratford was the farthest west James had been at that point.

It took a few years for him to find his footing in British Columbia. His first job was at the storied Raintree Restaurant, the first to introduce local, seasonal food to Vancouverites. He also picked fruit in the Okanagan and oversaw the food program of a college on Vancouver Island before landing in the kitchen at Sooke Harbour House. "What Sinclair Philip and the Sooke Harbour House did for me was incredible," he says. "We'd hand-write a new menu every day based on what was coming in." He was introduced not only to ingredients he'd never seen before but also to new ways of using the ones he did know. It was a standard that he would bring to Araxi when he moved to Whistler in 1997.

Given carte blanche to rebuild Araxi's kitchen and to change its entire concept from Italian to local and seasonal, James rose to the challenge.

"It was a little precious at first," he says of his early, tweezer-precise presentations, but once he'd forged relationships with the farmers and artisanal producers up and down the Sea-to-Sky Corridor (the area around what was then known less romantically as Highway 99) and throughout the Pemberton Valley, he quickly found his groove. "Product was key," he remembers with emphasis. Letting the ingredients shine on their own was paramount.

That first year, awards followed accolades, and James was invited to prepare a dinner at the prestigious James Beard House in New York City, where he and his crew received a standing ovation. He was just 28 years old. Since then, James, his wife and his two children have made their home among the farmers and producers in the Pemberton Valley. He's left only twice for any length of time: once to lead the kitchen when Toptable opened the sister restaurant Blue Water Cafe in Vancouver (2000–03), and once to cook at the Canadian Embassy in Rome (2005).

In 2010, with the Winter Olympics in Whistler, Araxi found itself representing Canada to customers from around the world with very high expectations. Meeting them was a monumental task; Araxi exceeded them. And what of future challenges? He's deeply involved in Toptable's latest projects, namely The Cellar by Araxi and Bar Oso, both of which are new to Whistler Village.

A perennial student of everything BC might bring to his table, James also watches with pride as young chefs he's mentored garner praise for their own achievements. A few have even moved on to open very successful restaurants of their own (and though he may not want to be reminded of it, two children of past employees recently joined his own kitchen's ranks). By way of a passion for local ingredients and a genuine respect for how those ingredients are prepared, he has helped to explore and define British Columbia's cuisine, thus inspiring future generations of cooks, both amateur and professional, not to follow in his footsteps but to make their own.

in the

KITCHEN

Executive sous chef MARK MCLOUGHLIN has spent most of his career in the kitchen at Araxi, working his way up from chef de partie through two long tours of duty. He is like a rock when the restaurant is at its very busiest, his unflappable steadfastness likely attributable to his devotion to fishing.

After studying at George Brown College Chef School in Toronto, pastry chef AARON HEATH started at Araxi in 1996, the year before his neighbour James Walt joined. James considers him "my fourth brother," since they've toiled side by side for so long and share an affinity for local, natural flavours and refined, exacting techniques. When he's not working, Aaron builds bikes and rock climbs.

in the
DINING ROOM

Glasgow-born **NEIL HENDERSON** (*centre*) landed at Araxi in 1992 by way of Edinburgh (where he earned a business degree), the French Alps (where he first acquired a taste for the resort life) and New Zealand (where he spent a season making wine). As the restaurant director, he is all precision and personality and his penchant for order and professionalism (possibly attributable to a childhood desire to join the Royal Marines) is softly expressed. Echoing that grace and cordiality are Araxi's three restaurant managers. Charming, with a refined palate for wine and a lifelong love of the outdoors, **PAT ALLAN** (*left*) came to Araxi from Alberta's Fairmont Chateau Lake Louise in 2002. The ebullient **TOVA JOHNSON** (*facing inset*), a "passionate firecracker" originally from Revelstoke, arrived in 2006 by way of several award-winning restaurants and brings an unrelenting enthusiasm to the team. **DARIN NEWTON** (*right*), a backcountry skier and certified climbing guide originally from Ontario, is the newest member. He offers a calm but engaging and charismatic brand of hospitality buttressed by a knowledge of wine that belies his years. Like Neil and Pat, he is a member of the International Sommelier Guild.

Master shucker PATRICK CANTIN-GAYTON has held capable court for the past three years, since his arrival from Montreal's highly regarded Les 400 Coups. There is a machine-like rhythm to his proceedings, a likely consequence of his zeal for woodworking, a skill he learned from his father. Eschewing store-bought oyster shuckers, Patrick crafted his own. He also built the oyster board he uses at the restaurant.

at the busy
oyster bar

17

in the
WINE CELLAR

In addition to being a talented musician (she plays the clarinet and the bass trombone), avid mountain biker and certified snowboard coach, wine director SAMANTHA RAHN is one of the most widely respected palates in Canada. She trained in Banff, where she presided over the list at the award-winning Maple Leaf Grill for six years. Since her 2007 arrival at Araxi, she has received several awards and accolades, including Sommelier of the Year at the Vancouver International Wine Festival in 2013.

Assisting Samantha with the 11,000-bottle cellar is former Vancouverite JASON KAWAGUCHI, who moved to Whistler 16 years ago after spending a sunny afternoon on Araxi's patio with a bottle of champagne and thinking to himself, "I think I might want to live here." After starting a family, pursuing a career in real estate and hiking to Mt. Everest base camp and back, he was drawn back to Araxi in 2009. Since then he has progressed into management and found passion in his continuing study of wine.

overseeing

THE BAR

Family man and bar manager RENE WUETHRICH has been a fixture at Araxi for more than 15 years. Trained in Zurich, Lausanne, Zermatt and Villars, Switzerland, he presides over an impressive collection of spirits, among them wide selections of single malt whiskies and bourbons. "If it needs to get done," says James, "Rene just gets it done." Though ever dependable, Rene is seldom found far from his wife and children in his time off, relishing every aspect of life in the mountains with them.

JASON REDMOND held front-of-house positions in Australia and on Vancouver Island before joining Araxi as the assistant bar manager in 2013. A commanding presence at the bar, as well as on the volleyball court where he's an original member of Whistler's outdoor league, he now brings his creative cocktails and considerable bartending skills to the role of bar manager at Araxi's sister venue Bar Oso.

the
RECIPES

shoots

BARELY TWENTY YEARS ago, the first signs of spring heralded an "off season," when the mountains in Whistler largely returned to the locals and the long wait for the following season's fresh powder would begin. Today beer festivals, golf tournaments, team endurance races, yoga celebrations, outdoor concerts and farmers' markets draw more annual visitors in the warmer months than the snow does in the winter.

While mountain bikes and skateboards supplant skis and snowboards, all attention remains fixed on the outdoors, where the transformations are especially vivid—and often delicious. Fresh halibut and sweet spot prawns sourced from British Columbia waters start off the season's bounty in April and May, followed by a summer of salmon. From the local soils emerge salad greens, fresh herbs, a variety of vegetables and legumes (carrots, beets, radishes, beans, peas and more), and lesser-known edibles like squash blossoms and green strawberries. The diversity is astounding.

With the heat of summer come the fresh Okanagan Valley fruits like peaches, cherries and pears (to the delight of pastry chef Aaron Heath) and the Pemberton Valley's juicy heirloom tomatoes. And past the farms, the meadows and valleys of the entire Sea-to-Sky Corridor—from Vancouver's North Shore through Squamish and beyond Pemberton to the outskirts of tiny hamlets like D'Arcy and Devine—are a forager's delight. If one knows where to look, as the cooks at Araxi do, wild ginger, morels, fiddlehead ferns and ramps are everywhere—and often on the menu.

menu

COCKTAILS

Otro Loco Mas   *Peach Sangria*

Blue Bird   *Truth & Lies*

26-29

SMALL

30 Quinoa & Spring
Vegetable Salad

33 Spot Prawn Sashimi
with Fresh Herb Glaze

34 Small Shrimp in
Barbecued Avocado

36 Dungeness Crab in Egg
Crepe with Yuzu Gel

39 Grilled Wild Scallop
Brochettes with
Summer Vegetables

42 Scallop Carpaccio
with Basil & Helen's Oil

44 Albacore Tuna
"Niçoise" Salad Sticks

46 Wild Salmon
Tartare with Seaweed

48 Hot-Smoked Chinook
Salmon & Marinated
Watermelon

50 Sockeye Salmon
Chirashi

52 Roasted Roma Tomato
Soup with Grilled
Cheese Garnish

53 Confit Heirloom
Tomatoes & Burrata

54 Peperonata with
Buffalo Mozzarella

LARGER

56 Roasted Prawns
with Curry Dressing

59 Grilled Neon Squid
with Salsify

60 Chilled Poached
Salmon with
Cucumber & Yogurt

63 Stinging Nettle
Gnocchi & King Crab

67 Chorizo-Crusted
Lingcod with
Tomato Fondue

70 Flaked Lingcod
"Chowder" with
Broccoli

74 Spot Prawn, Corn
& Herb Risotto

76 Duck Egg Pasta
Tortellini with Duck
Confit Filling

79 Pork Jowls with
Asparagus & Peas

82 Romy's Chicken
under the Brick

85 Spiced Lamb
Meatballs "Bar Oso"

DESSERTS

88 Lavender Meringues
with Blueberries &
Mint

92 Triple Chocolate
Cookies

93 Buttermilk
Panna Cotta with
Strawberries

94 Cherry Ice Cream Bars

98 Warm Chocolate Tart
with Blackberries

100 Orange Marshmallow
& Chocolate Treats

shoots

This cocktail is a twist on a Mojito and is named from a line in an Ernest Hemingway story titled "A Clean, Well-Lighted Place." Be sure to use an unsweetened apple juice.

otro loco mas | MAKES 6

honey syrup

4 oz honey

4 oz very hot water

cocktail

12 oz organic pure cloudy apple juice (we use Santa Cruz)

6 oz reposado tequila (we use Herradura)

6 oz Spanish brandy (we use Torres)

4 oz fresh lemon juice

4 oz Honey Syrup (recipe below)

40 to 50 fresh mint leaves

6 oz club soda or sparkling mineral water

HONEY SYRUP Place the honey in a measuring cup, pour the hot water over it and stir until the honey is dissolved. Refrigerate until well chilled.

COCKTAIL Have ready 6 Collins glasses, each half-full of ice cubes. Half-fill a large jug with ice cubes. Add the apple juice, tequila, brandy, lemon juice and honey syrup and stir until well chilled. Strain the mixture into individual glasses.

Place 7 or 8 mint leaves in the palm of one hand. With the flat of your other hand, slap the mint 2 to 3 times to release the oils. Add the mint to one glass and stir gently. Top with 1 oz of soda (or sparkling water) and more ice, if required. Repeat with the remaining mint and soda.

peach sangria | MAKES 6

1 bottle (750 mL/3 cups) rosé wine

6 oz peach purée

4 oz Triple Sec

4 oz peach liqueur

4 oz elderflower cordial

2 cups ice cubes

6 oz sparkling wine (Cava is a great value)

3 cups chopped seasonal fruit (e.g. peaches, nectarines, apple, oranges and blueberries for colour), for garnish

Have ready 6 white wine glasses. In a pitcher, combine the wine, peach purée, Triple Sec, peach liqueur and elderflower cordial over the ice and stir until well chilled. Fill each glass with ice, add $\frac{1}{6}$ of the mixed alcohol and top with 1 oz sparkling wine. Garnish each glass with fresh seasonal fruit.

blue bird | MAKES 6

12 oz fresh grapefruit juice
10 oz pisco
3 oz fresh lime juice
2 oz blue curaçao
2 oz maraschino liqueur
2 cups ice cubes
6 Amarena cherries, for garnish

Chill 6 martini glasses in the freezer.
In a pitcher, combine all of the liquid
ingredients over the ice and stir until
well chilled. Strain the mixture into
the martini glasses and garnish with
an Amarena cherry.

This drink is nice with a little bubble or carbonation. At the restaurant we carbonate our own drinks, but club soda will give you the same effervescence at home without compromising the flavour, as the recipe is already more concentrated.

truth & lies | MAKES 6

lavender-infused simple syrup
1 cup Simple Syrup (page 219)
½ cup dried lavender

cocktail
12 oz fresh grapefruit juice
10 oz vodka
4 oz Cointreau
3 oz fresh lime juice
3 oz Lavender-infused Simple Syrup (recipe below)
Ice cubes to chill
6 oz club soda (optional)
6 slices, strips or pieces grapefruit zest, for garnish

LAVENDER-INFUSED SIMPLE SYRUP
Bring the simple syrup to a boil on high heat, add the lavender and continue boiling for 1 minute. Remove from the heat and allow to cool. Use the syrup once cooled, or ideally, once steeped overnight (no need to strain the lavender). This will keep refrigerated in an airtight container for up to 2 weeks.

COCKTAIL Have ready 6 coupe glasses. In a pitcher, combine the grapefruit juice, vodka, Cointreau, lime juice and simple syrup over the ice and stir until well chilled. Pour in the club soda (if using). Strain the mixture into individual coupe glasses without ice. Garnish with a twist of grapefruit zest.

29

SERVES
4 TO 6
AS PART
OF AN
APPETIZER
PLATTER

quinoa & spring vegetable salad

QUINOA Place the quinoa in a fine-mesh sieve and run it under cold water for a minute or so to rinse it and then set aside.

In a small saucepan with a tight-fitting lid, heat the olive oil on medium heat. Add the onion and cook until softened and translucent, 4 to 5 minutes. Stir in the quinoa and sauté for 2 minutes. Add the vegetable nage, increase the heat to high and bring to a boil. Immediately turn down the heat to low and cover the pot. Cook for 20 minutes.

Remove the pot from the heat and let it stand, still covered, in a warm place for 10 minutes. Lift the lid. All the liquid should have evaporated and the grains should be tender. (Drain off any excess moisture.) Season to taste with salt. Arrange the quinoa in a shallow bowl and refrigerate, covered, until cool.

OLIVE OIL AND CHIVE VINAIGRETTE In a small bowl, whisk together the olive oil, vinegar, honey, chives and salt until well combined. Set aside. This will keep refrigerated in an airtight container for up to 3 or 4 days.

quinoa

1½ cups uncooked quinoa (red or white)

2 Tbsp extra-virgin olive oil

1 small onion, minced

3 cups Vegetable Nage (page 220)

Sea salt to taste

olive oil and chive vinaigrette

1 cup extra-virgin olive oil

¼ cup apple or maple vinegar

1 Tbsp honey

1 Tbsp chopped fresh chives

Pinch of sea salt

This very tasty seasonal salad can be used as part of an appetizer platter or as part of a picnic-style meal in a field or in your garden. In the fall, you could make it with roasted root vegetables. Look for the very fruity and sweet apple or maple vinegars at fine grocers.

SPRING VEGETABLE SALAD Set a serving platter in the fridge to chill. Fill a large bowl with ice water and set aside.

Bring a medium pot of lightly salted water to a boil on high heat. Add the asparagus and cook for 2 minutes. Using a slotted spoon, transfer the asparagus to the bowl of ice water to stop the cooking. Reserve the boiling water. Transfer the cooled asparagus to a plate and set aside.

Bring the water in the pot back to a boil. Add the peas and cook for 2 minutes. Quickly drain the peas and plunge them into the ice water to stop the cooking. When the peas are cool, drain the ice water.

TO SERVE To the bowl of quinoa, add ½ cup of the vinaigrette and stir until well combined. Arrange the quinoa evenly across the chilled platter. Top with the asparagus, peas, tomatoes, cucumber spears, watercress and pecans. Drizzle with the remaining vinaigrette. Serve immediately.

spring vegetable salad

18 asparagus spears, fibrous ends trimmed

2 cups whole snap peas, strings removed

2 cups cherry tomato halves

4 baby cucumbers, skin on, cut into quarters lengthwise

1 cup watercress leaves

½ cup pecan halves, toasted

IT'S NOT HARD to get along with Jesse Fromowitz at GoodField Farms. Araxi's cooks love his down-to-earth character, as he's not afraid to try new things and truly loves getting his hands dirty. Jesse is all about natural foods, growing arugula, peas, heirloom tomatoes, garlic, sunchokes, beets, a variety of chili peppers and more with a dedication underpinned by a sincere and infectious affection for the soil. Chef James Walt is especially drawn to Jesse's microgreens, particularly his pea shoots, basil and radish. These typically appear as garnishes complementing spring seafoods like fresh halibut and spot prawns. Jesse's dreadlocked brother, Elliot, is also a natural farmer, and supplies the restaurant on occasion through his own Manna Farm, located nearby in the fertile Birken Valley. Both are regulars at the Whistler Farmers Market.

spot prawn sashimi with fresh herb glaze

On the West Coast, spot prawns signal the start of the spring fishing season and all of the good things to come. If you are unable to find spot prawns, try fresh raw scallops or rock prawns.

Using a sharp knife, gently slice lengthwise down the middle of each prawn tail, cutting about ¼ of the way through the flesh. (You do not want to separate the 2 halves.) With a small paring knife, remove and discard any of the dark vein-like intestinal tracts down the centre. Arrange the prawns on a large platter, gently pressing them open along the incision, and refrigerate the platter, uncovered, for 30 to 40 minutes. (The prawns should be very cold.)

In a blender or food processor, combine the parsley and chervil (or dill) with the canola (or safflower) oil, vinegar, lemon juice, salt and pepper and blend at high speed until smooth. Using a spoon or a pastry brush, evenly coat the prawns with this herb glaze. Drizzle with the sesame oil and garnish with the herb leaves. Serve immediately while very cold.

18 spot prawn tails, peeled, lightly rinsed under cold running water and then patted dry

2 Tbsp chopped flat-leaf parsley

1 Tbsp coarsely chopped fresh chervil or dill

¼ cup canola or safflower oil

2 Tbsp rice vinegar

Juice of 1 lemon

½ tsp sea salt

½ tsp crushed black pepper

1 Tbsp good-quality toasted sesame oil

¼ cup micro herbs or fresh herbs (parsley and chervil are good)

The first time I grilled an avocado was an epiphany. Here, their grilled flavour and creamy texture perfectly complement the shrimp. These are quick to prepare when friends stop by unexpectedly—just try to use avocados that aren't too firm.

small shrimp in barbecued avocado

Preheat your barbecue or indoor grill to high heat. (Be sure that it is well cleaned.) Set a small bowl in the fridge to chill.

Cut each avocado in half lengthwise. Give a light twist to each avocado and, using your knife or a spoon, gently remove the pit. Arrange the avocado halves on a baking tray, flesh side up.

In a small bowl, whisk 2 Tbsp of the olive oil with the pinch of salt and pepper and the lemon juice and zest until blended. Pour this marinade evenly over the avocado flesh, then turn the avocados over and move them around the tray to further coat the flesh with marinade.

Using tongs, carefully brush the barbecue (or indoor grill) with a lightly oiled rag or kitchen towel to prevent sticking. Place the avocados on the grill, flesh side down, for 2 to 3 minutes, until nicely charred and slightly softened. They will continue to cook once removed from the grill (we call this residual heat). Transfer the avocados to a serving platter, skin side up, and let stand for 5 to 10 minutes to cool slightly.

In the chilled bowl, very gently combine the shrimp, mayonnaise and chives with the ½ tsp of salt until well mixed. Be careful not to break the shrimp. Check the seasoning.

TO SERVE Spoon some of the shrimp mixture into the middle of each barbecued avocado half and drizzle with the remaining 1 Tbsp olive oil. Serve immediately.

5 large avocados, just ripe

3 Tbsp extra-virgin olive oil

½ tsp + 1 good pinch of sea salt

1 good pinch of cracked black pepper

Juice and zest of 1 lemon

18 oz Matane or other good-quality small fresh shrimp, cooked

½ cup Yuzu Mayonnaise (page 219)

1 Tbsp chopped fresh chives

MAKES
8 ROLLS
(SERVES 8
AS AN
APPETIZER
OR MORE AS
A CANAPÉ)

dungeness crab in egg crepe with yuzu gel

EGG CREPE (TAMAGO) In a medium bowl, combine all of the ingredients and mix with a fork until blended. Strain the mixture through a fine-mesh sieve into a clean bowl and refrigerate for 30 minutes.

Heat a nonstick crepe pan on medium-low heat. Ladle about 2 Tbsp of the egg mixture into the pan, then swirl it to cover the entire surface. Let cook until set, about 2 minutes, and then transfer to a clean plate. Repeat with the remaining egg batter. (You should have about 20 crepes.)

YUZU GEL Have ready an 8 to 10-inch pie plate or dish. Place the simple syrup in a small saucepan on medium heat. Whisk in the agar agar, bring to a boil, then turn down the heat to a light simmer for 3 minutes, whisking occasionally. The syrup will thicken to a consistency similar to a mayonnaise. Remove from the heat and whisk in the yuzu juice. Strain the mixture through a fine-mesh sieve into the pie plate (or dish) and refrigerate for about 1 hour, until firmly set.

Using a dull knife or a spoon, cut the firm gel into roughly ½-inch cubes and transfer them to a blender or food processor. Process at low speed, then increase the speed to high to achieve as smooth a gel as possible (add 1 Tbsp simple syrup, if necessary, to achieve smoothness). Press the gel through a fine-mesh sieve into a small bowl and refrigerate until needed.

egg crepe (tamago)
5 whole eggs
1 egg yolk
3½ Tbsp mirin
2½ Tbsp shiro dashi
1 Tbsp light soy sauce

yuzu gel
1 cup Simple Syrup (page 219)
1 tsp agar agar
1 cup yuzu juice

This recipe is an Araxi classic that pairs the sweetness of local Dungeness crab with smoked salmon and floral, citrusy yuzu. You can find yuzu juice and shiro dashi at most Japanese grocers; look for agar agar in the baking section of most fine grocers. Halving the crepe recipe is not recommended, so freeze the extra crepes in a resealable plastic bag. They are delicious with other savoury fillings or thinly sliced and served in soups or on top of salads.

DUNGENESS CRAB IN EGG CREPE Fill a large bowl with ice. Set the crabmeat in a bowl over the ice, add the yuzu mayonnaise and chives, and mix gently and thoroughly.

To assemble the rolls, place an egg crepe on a cutting board. Place 4 oz crabmeat (you can weigh and form it into balls) near the bottom of the crepe, and, using a palette knife, spread it evenly across the bottom third of the crepe. Arrange 2 slices of smoked salmon over the crab, top with 4 pieces of avocado and cover with ⅛ of the shiso (or arugula). Starting at the bottom edge, very gently roll up the crepe, enclosing the filling as tightly as possible (the crepe is delicate, so be careful not to rip it). When you have about 1 inch left to roll, spread a very thin layer of yuzu gel across the top of the crepe and continue rolling to seal the crepe completely. Transfer the roll to a plate and refrigerate it while you make the rest. (You will have some avocado left over.)

TO SERVE Slice each crepe in half widthwise, then place the halves side by side (this makes them easier to slice) and cut them into thirds for 6 pieces. Repeat with the remaining rolls. Set the pieces on individual plates or a serving platter and garnish each one with an orange segment and a little yuzu gel. Serve immediately.

dungeness crab in egg crepe

2 lb fresh Dungeness crabmeat, picked of shells or cartilage

½ cup Yuzu Mayonnaise (page 219)

1 Tbsp chopped fresh chives

8 Egg Crepes (see opposite)

16 slices cold-smoked salmon (we use Nanuk brand sockeye)

3 ripe avocados, each halved, pitted, peeled and cut into 12 pieces

8 shiso or arugula leaves, roughly torn

1 recipe Yuzu Gel (see opposite)

2 mandarin oranges, segmented

DUNGENESS CRAB
IN EGG CREPE
WITH YUZU GEL
page 36

GRILLED WILD SCALLOP
BROCHETTES WITH
SUMMER VEGETABLES
page 40

grilled wild scallop brochettes with summer vegetables

Have ready a bowl of ice water and a clean kitchen towel. Bring a medium pot of lightly salted water to a boil on high heat. Add the pattypan and zucchini to the pot and boil for 1 minute. Using a slotted spoon, transfer them to the ice water to stop the cooking. Transfer to the kitchen towel to drain. Reserve the boiling water.

Add the bell peppers to the boiling water and cook for 1 minute. Using the slotted spoon, transfer them to the ice water to cool and then to the kitchen towel to drain. Repeat with the peas (cook for 1 minute), followed by the onion (cook for 2 minutes).

Fill a baking tray or roasting pan with ice. Have ready a large serving platter in the fridge. Arrange the pattypan and zucchini, red and yellow bell peppers, peas and onions in separate piles on a plate and set them over the ice. Place the scallops on a plate and set it over the ice too. Assemble the skewers one at a time, threading the ingredients in an order such as the following to maximize the flavours: 1 piece of pattypan, 1 piece of red bell pepper, 1 piece of onion, 1 scallop, 1 piece of zucchini, 1 snap pea, 1 piece of yellow bell pepper, 1 piece of onion, 1 scallop, 1 piece of pattypan, 1 piece of red bell pepper, 1 piece of onion, 1 scallop, 1 snap pea,

6 pattypan squash, cut in half widthwise and separated

6 baby zucchini, cut in half lengthwise and separated

1 red bell pepper, seeds removed, cut into ½-inch cubes

1 yellow bell pepper, seeds removed, cut into ½-inch cubes

12 snap peas

1 large red onion, cut into ½-inch cubes and separated

18 medium wild Pacific scallops, chilled

2 Tbsp extra-virgin olive oil

Sea salt to taste

1 Tbsp toasted sesame oil

6 bamboo skewers, each 6 to 8 inches long

These versatile brochettes are a great summer dish: substitute salmon or prawns for the scallops, if you like, and try variations with eggplant, tomatoes and even blanched corn on the cob. Serve the brochettes with salad for a full meal. Before you begin this recipe, soak six bamboo skewers, each six to eight inches long, in cold water for half an hour to prevent them from burning on the barbecue.

1 piece of zucchini and 1 piece yellow pepper. (For each brochette, you will use 4 pieces of bell pepper (2 red, 2 yellow), 3 scallops, 2 pieces of pattypan, 2 pieces of zucchini, 2 snap peas and 3 pieces of red onion.) Place the skewers on the platter in the fridge as you complete them.

Preheat the barbecue or indoor grill to high heat. Brush the grill with a lightly oiled towel just before cooking to avoid sticking. Brush the brochettes with the olive oil and season evenly with salt. Place on the hot grill and cook for about 2 minutes, then turn the brochettes over and cook for a further 2 minutes until the scallops are lightly charred and firmed up. Remove from the heat and let stand for 2 minutes to rest. Drizzle with the toasted sesame oil.

The olive oil makes all the difference in this recipe. We use the fantastic Golden Olive "Eleni" extra-virgin olive oil that Basil and Helen Koutalianos of Basil Olive Oil Products in Maple Ridge, BC, produce from their olive grove in Greece. If you can't find this particular oil, use a good-quality very fruity extra-virgin olive oil instead.

scallop carpaccio with basil & helen's oil

Using a sharp knife, carefully slice the scallops into 3 to 4 slices each. Arrange the slices evenly among 4 plates, trying not to overlap them too much. Cover with plastic wrap and refrigerate to keep them as cold as possible.

Just before serving, whisk together the olive oil and lime juice in a small bowl. Divide the tomatoes and oranges evenly over the scallops on each of the 4 plates. Gently tear the basil leaves and arrange them over the scallops. Drizzle with the olive oil, romesco sauce and vinaigrette, trying to evenly coat the scallops. Lightly season with salt and white pepper and serve immediately.

12 large very fresh wild Pacific scallops

¼ cup good-quality extra-virgin olive oil

2 Tbsp fresh lime juice

6 cherry tomatoes, thinly sliced

2 oranges, peeled and cut into segments

20 large basil leaves

2 Tbsp Romesco Sauce (page 221)

Pinch of sea salt

Pinch of cracked white pepper

albacore tuna "niçoise" salad sticks

These skewers make a great canapé for a summer party. They look more interesting if they are different, so have fun when it comes time to assemble them and change them up as you go. Serve them on regular bamboo skewers or dress them up by using decorative cocktail sticks.

Heat a nonstick pan on high heat. (Do not add oil.) Add the tuna loin and sear for about 30 seconds on each side, until lightly golden. Transfer the tuna to a plate and refrigerate, uncovered, until cool.

Have ready a kitchen scale, a chilled plate and a ½-inch round cookie cutter. Using a clean, sharp knife, cut the tuna into ½-inch cubes, each 1 oz in weight. (You should have 18 cubes.) Transfer the tuna to the chilled plate and refrigerate, covered.

Bring a small pot of lightly salted water to a boil. Using a slotted spoon, gently lower the quail eggs into the pot. Cook for 2 minutes and 45 seconds and remove, immediately submerging the eggs in ice water. After 5 minutes, remove from the water and peel off the shells. Store in the refrigerator until needed.

Bring a new pot of lightly salted water to a boil on medium-high heat. Slice the potatoes lengthwise into ¼-inch-wide rounds. Using the cookie cutter, cut at least 18 small rounds from the potato slices. Drop the potatoes into the pot of boiling water and cook until just tender, 4 to 5 minutes. (Watch them closely so they do not overcook!) Using a slotted spoon, transfer the potatoes to a plate and refrigerate, uncovered, to cool completely. Reserve the pot of boiling water.

Fill a large bowl with ice water. Cut the green beans into ¾-inch pieces, add them to the boiling water and cook for 2 minutes. Using a slotted spoon, transfer the beans to the ice water to stop the cooking. Drain and set aside.

Fill a baking tray or roasting pan with ice. Have ready a large serving platter in the fridge. Cut the eggs in half, lengthwise. Arrange the eggs, potatoes, beans, tomatoes, anchovies and olives in separate piles on a plate and set them over the ice. Remove the tuna from the fridge and set it over the ice too. Assemble the skewers one at a time, threading some of each ingredient onto each one and ending with the tuna. Place the skewers on the platter in the fridge as you complete them.

Just before serving, drizzle the platter with salsa verde and sprinkle the tuna with salt. Pass around the platter, keeping it as cold as possible.

18 oz centre-cut sashimi-grade albacore tuna loin

9 quail eggs

2 large unpeeled yellow-fleshed potatoes (Yukon Gold are great)

10 large green beans

20 baby heirloom or cherry tomatoes

1 small can (3 oz, or about 20 fillets) marinated white anchovies, drained

20 pitted Niçoise or small black olives

1 cup Salsa Verde (page 166)

18 small bamboo skewers or decorative cocktail sticks

1 tsp coarse sea salt

wild salmon tartare with seaweed

Use ocean-caught sockeye or chinook salmon for this tartare. As you are eating it raw, freshness is key. Remember, fish shouldn't smell fishy. Alternatively, look for sushi-grade salmon in fine grocers or at your local fish-monger. Marinated wakame seaweed with sesame is common in Japanese markets and nicely complements the tartare. The tartare is also great on its own.

CHILI-YUZU MARINADE In a small bowl, whisk together the vinegar, grapeseed oil, chili paste, soy sauce and lemon and yuzu juices until well combined. Set aside. This will keep refrigerated in an airtight container for up to 3 days.

WILD SALMON TARTARE Fill a large bowl with ice and place a smaller stainless steel bowl on top.

Place the salmon on a very clean work surface and, using a sharp knife, cut the salmon widthwise into very thin slices. Cut the slices into long thin strips and then cut these strips crosswise into tiny minced cubes. Transfer the salmon to the bowl set over ice. Add the bell and jalapeño peppers, green onions, chives and 5 Tbsp chili-yuzu marinade. Season with a pinch of sea salt and mix gently until thoroughly combined.

Place a 3-inch ring mould (or cookie cutter) in the centre of a serving plate. Spoon 2 Tbsp of seaweed salad into the mould, spreading it into an even layer. Top with ¼ of the salmon mixture and gently pack it down. Carefully remove the mould. Repeat this process until each plate has a layered round of seaweed and salmon.

TO SERVE Garnish each plate with cucumber slices and drizzle the tartare with a tablespoon of the chili-yuzu marinade. Serve immediately.

chili-yuzu marinade

¼ cup rice wine vinegar

2 Tbsp grapeseed oil

2 Tbsp amarillo chili paste (Peruvian chili paste available at fine grocers)

2 Tbsp soy sauce

1 Tbsp fresh lemon juice

2 tsp yuzu juice (available at Japanese grocers)

wild salmon tartare

12 oz fresh skinless, boneless wild salmon fillet, well chilled

¼ cup minced green bell pepper

1 Tbsp minced red jalapeño pepper, seeds removed

¼ cup chopped green onions, white and green parts

1 Tbsp chopped fresh chives

½ cup sesame-marinated wakame seaweed salad (available at Japanese grocers)

Pinch of sea salt

1 large English cucumber, skin on, sliced into very thin rounds

hot-smoked chinook salmon & marinated watermelon

Start this recipe the day before you plan to serve it so the salmon has time to marinate overnight. For best results, have your smoker ready (or make one using a roasting pan, cooling rack or perforated pan and two cups of apple, cherry or alderwood wood chips, which are available at local hardware stores).

HOT-SMOKED SALMON Have ready a shallow baking dish just large enough to hold the salmon. Cut an 11 × 18-inch piece of plastic wrap and place it in the bottom of the dish, allowing the edges of the plastic wrap to hang over the sides of the dish.

In a small bowl, combine the sugar, salt and citrus zests. Sprinkle ⅓ of this mixture evenly over the plastic wrap, then place the salmon, skin side down, on top. Using a pastry brush, baste the fish with the gin (or vodka) and cover it with the remaining sugar/salt mixture. Fold the edges of the plastic wrap tightly over the salmon, making sure the fish is completely sealed. Refrigerate for 12 hours, turn the wrapped salmon over and refrigerate for another 6 hours.

MARINATED WATERMELON Using a large melon baller, scoop out as many melon balls as you can (about 50) and place them in a bowl. Cut and discard the rind from the remaining melon but reserve the flesh. Place the watermelon flesh in a blender and purée until smooth.

Using a fine-mesh sieve, strain the melon purée over the melon balls. Pour in the gin, elderflower cordial and ginger, mix gently and refrigerate for at least 4 hours or (best) overnight.

continued overleaf

hot-smoked salmon

½ cup granulated sugar

¼ cup kosher salt

Zest of 1 lemon

Zest of 1 orange

Zest of 1 lime

2 lb fresh, skin-on chinook salmon fillet (or substitute sockeye or coho)

½ oz gin or vodka

1 Tbsp extra-virgin olive oil

¼ cup sour cream

¼ cup dill, chervil or tarragon sprigs

marinated watermelon

½ medium seedless watermelon

½ cup gin

¼ cup elderflower cordial (Ikea is a good source)

1 Tbsp grated fresh ginger

FINISH SALMON Carefully remove and discard the plastic wrap from the salmon. Rinse the fish under cold water and gently pat it dry with paper towels. Return the salmon to the baking dish and refrigerate, uncovered, for at least 2 more hours to allow the skin to set.

Meanwhile, set up your smoker according to its instructions or create a stovetop version using a roasting pan with a tight-fitting lid (you will also need a cooling rack (or a perforated tray) that fits inside it). Place 2 cups of wood chips in a large bowl, cover with water and let soak for at least 30 minutes.

Drain the soaked wood chips and mound in the centre of the roasting pan. Using a torch, light the chips. Once the flames have subsided and the chips start to smoke, place the cooling rack (or perforated tray) in the roasting pan or turn your smoker to low (or no) heat. Remove the salmon from the fridge, cut it into six 5-oz portions and place it on the rack in your smoker. Cover and smoke for 20 to 25 minutes. Refrigerate the smoked fish until needed.

Heat the olive oil on medium in a sauté pan large enough to hold the salmon. Add the salmon and cook, flesh side down, for 2 minutes until golden brown. Turn the fish over and remove the pan from the heat.

TO SERVE Place a piece of salmon in the centre of each plate. Arrange some of the watermelon balls around the salmon and garnish with the fresh herbs and sour cream.

sockeye salmon chirashi

Chirashi, which means "scattered," is a nice sushi-type meal without all of the rolling and shaping. You can use various vegetables and seafood and have fun with various combinations. You will need a rice cooker to prepare this dish; they are so handy that every household should have one, so if you don't have one, go get one!

SUSHI RICE Place the rice and 2 cups of water in a large bowl. Using your hands, swirl the rice in the water and press it against the bowl in a circular motion to remove any excess starch. Drain the rice in a fine-mesh sieve. Repeat this rinsing and draining process until the water runs clear and no starch remains. Drain the rice one last time, removing as much water as possible.

Transfer the rice to a rice cooker, add 2 cups of clean water and set the machine to "cook." Once the rice is cooked, the switch will turn to "keep warm." Let the rice rest in this mode for 10 minutes.

While the rice is resting, prepare the sushi-zu (the finished rice vinegar). In a small nonreactive saucepan on medium heat, combine the rice wine vinegar, sugar and salt, bring them to a boil and then remove from the heat.

Scoop the rice into a large wooden bowl. Sprinkle the sushi-zu over the rice. With a rice paddle, fold the sushi-zu into the rice using cutting motions and being careful not to crush the rice grains. Once the sushi-zu is finally incorporated, fan the rice with a magazine or a fan to cool it down to just slightly warm as quickly as possible. The rice will become firm as it cools, so you don't want it to cool too much.

SALMON CHIRASHI Have ready 6 slightly damp bowls. Divide the rice evenly among the bowls and sprinkle with the sesame seeds. Arrange 3 shiso (or basil) leaves on top of the rice in each bowl, followed by 2 slices of smoked salmon, 4 pieces of avocado and 1/6 of the cucumbers.

Using a very sharp, very clean knife, halve the salmon fillet lengthwise. Slice each half into 9 pieces, for a total of 18. Place 3 pieces in each bowl, then garnish with the daikon radish, salmon caviar and ginger (if using).

TO SERVE Divide the soy sauce among 6 small ramekins or dipping bowls and serve alongside the chirashi. Guests can drizzle a little soy over their chirashi or dip the fish as they eat it.

sushi rice

2 cups uncooked sushi rice
¼ cup rice wine vinegar
¼ cup granulated sugar
2 tsp salt

salmon chirashi

4 cups cooked sushi rice, warm
1 Tbsp toasted sesame seeds
12 shiso or basil leaves
12 slices cold-smoked sockeye salmon
3 ripe avocados, halved, pitted, peeled and each cut into 8 pieces (24 pieces total)
1 English cucumber, skin on, sliced into thin rounds
18 oz skinless, boneless sashimi-grade sockeye salmon fillet
1 cup thinly sliced daikon radish
3 Tbsp sushi-grade salmon caviar
¼ cup pickled ginger (optional)
¼ cup good-quality soy sauce

This soup is an Araxi favourite. The key is to give the tomatoes some charred flavour by roasting (or smoking or even grilling) them. And remember, hot soup calls for hot bowls to serve it in.

roasted roma tomato soup with grilled cheese garnish

ROASTED ROMA TOMATO SOUP Preheat the oven to 400°F. Arrange the tomatoes, cut side down, on a baking tray. Drizzle with 3 Tbsp of the olive oil, season with salt and bake for 15 to 20 minutes, or until the skins start to char and the tomatoes soften. If you prefer a smoky flavour, cook them for about 10 more minutes until the skins darken and the juices evaporate.

Pour the remaining olive oil into a large saucepan on medium heat. Add the onions, garlic and fennel and cook for 8 to 10 minutes, until softened and slightly coloured. Stir in the bouquet garni, tomato paste and sugar and cook for 3 to 4 minutes to release the flavours and cook the tomato paste. Add the canned tomatoes and juice, cook for 2 minutes, and then add the vegetable (or chicken) stock. Bring the soup to a boil, add the roasted tomatoes and all their juices and oils, and turn down the heat to a simmer for 8 to 10 minutes. Stir in the paprika and season with salt. Remove from the heat and pour in the cream, if using.

Working in batches if necessary, carefully transfer the soup to a blender or food processor and purée at high speed until smooth. Strain through a fine-mesh sieve and reserve until needed.

GRILLED CHEESE Preheat a panini press (or have ready a nonstick pan). Set 2 slices of bread on the counter and cover them with the cheese. Top with the remaining bread slices to make 2 filled sandwiches. (If you are using the nonstick pan, place it on medium-low heat now.)

Evenly butter the outer side of the bread on both sandwiches. Place the buttered sandwiches in the panini press or in the nonstick pan and cook until golden and the cheese has started to melt, 2 to 3 minutes. While hot and crispy, cut each sandwich into quarters.

TO SERVE Ladle the soup into heated bowls and garnish each serving with a piece of grilled cheese sandwich.

roasted roma tomato soup

15 fresh Roma tomatoes, cut in half

¾ cup extra-virgin olive oil, divided

Sea salt to taste

2 medium onions, sliced

4 cloves garlic, sliced

1 fennel bulb, sliced

1 bouquet garni (12 basil leaves, 2 sprigs of fresh rosemary, 2 bay leaves and 10 white peppercorns wrapped in cheesecloth or in a coffee filter secured with string)

½ cup tomato paste

⅓ cup granulated sugar

2 cans (each 28 fl oz) plum tomatoes

9 cups vegetable or chicken stock

1 Tbsp smoked paprika

⅔ cup whipping cream (optional)

grilled cheese

4 slices good-quality sandwich bread

6 oz aged cheddar (Avonlea Clothbound Cheddar is great), sliced ⅛ inch thick

2 Tbsp salted butter, softened

This is a great recipe to use up any slightly overripe garden tomatoes. Lightly cooking the heirlooms may seem like sacrilege, but it only accents their sweet flavour. Serve the tomatoes with some nice crusty bread to soak up all the goodness.

SERVES
4 TO 6
AS AN
APPETIZER
PLATTER

confit heirloom tomatoes & burrata

Place the olive oil and garlic in a high-sided medium saucepan and heat on low heat (use a deep-fat thermometer to check the heat of the oil: it should be 130 to 140°F). Cook the garlic for 30 minutes, until softened. Gently add the tomatoes to the warm oil, followed by the rosemary, thyme and bay leaves, and cook for 20 minutes. Remove the pot from the heat and let stand until cool.

Arrange the arugula around the outside edges of a serving platter. Place the burrata (still as whole as possible) in the centre. Using a slotted spoon, transfer the confit tomatoes and garlic to the platter, placing them around the burrata. Remove and discard the herb stems from the oil, then drizzle some of the flavoured oil over the platter. Sprinkle with salt and pepper.

2 cups good-quality extra-virgin olive oil

1 head fresh garlic, sliced in half horizontally (keep the outer papery layer on the garlic)

2 lb heirloom tomatoes (none larger than an average-sized orange), cores removed

2 sprigs rosemary

2 sprigs thyme

3 fresh bay leaves

2 cups arugula or light salad greens

1 lb burrata

Sea salt and cracked black pepper to taste

Crusty bread, to serve

Nothing says summer to me like this dish. The peperonata keeps well for three to four days and actually tastes better the day after it is prepared. Serve it with some good crusty bread and a quality buffalo mozzarella. Look for this soft cheese—we make some great ones here in Canada—in most cheese shops, deli counters or Italian grocers.

SERVES
4 TO 6
AS PART
OF AN
APPETIZER
PLATTER

peperonata with buffalo mozzarella

Heat the ⅓ cup olive oil in a medium saucepan on medium heat. Add the shallots and garlic and cook until softened and translucent, about 5 minutes. Stir in the peppers and cook until softened, 8 to 10 minutes, then add the vinegar, raisins and sugar. Cook until the vinegar has evaporated, 4 to 5 minutes, then remove from the heat and season with salt and pepper.

Once the peperonata has cooled, fold in the pine nuts and mint. Mix thoroughly and check the seasoning. Arrange the peperonata on a serving platter.

Place the buffalo mozzarella on the peppers, drizzle with the 3 Tbsp olive oil and the balsamic crema (or balsamic vinegar), and season with salt and pepper. Garnish with some fresh mint leaves and serve.

⅓ cup + 3 Tbsp extra-virgin olive oil

6 shallots, thinly sliced

2 cloves garlic, thinly sliced

3 large bell peppers (1 red, 1 yellow, 1 orange), seeds removed, thinly sliced

½ cup sherry vinegar

¼ cup raisins, soaked in warm water until plump, then strained

2 Tbsp granulated sugar

Sea salt and cracked black pepper to taste

¼ cup pine nuts, toasted

10 mint leaves, very thinly sliced

5 balls buffalo mozzarella, each 4 to 5 oz, cut into quarters

2 Tbsp balsamic crema or balsamic vinegar

2 sprigs fresh mint, for garnish

This is a great recipe for your own Longtable or picnic dinner served with other salads and vegetables. At Araxi we use sustainably harvested prawns certified by the Vancouver Aquarium's Ocean Wise program. Be sure to use the best-quality ocean-friendly prawns you can find.

SERVES
4 TO 6
AS PART
OF AN
ENTRÉE
PLATTER

roasted prawns with curry dressing

CURRY DRESSING In a small sauté pan, heat the grapeseed oil on medium-low heat and add the garlic, ginger and shallot. Cook for 3 to 4 minutes, or until softened and lightly coloured. Add the curry powder and cook for a further 2 minutes until it is toasted and clearly fragrant. Remove from the heat and allow to cool slightly.

In a blender, combine the curry mixture with the yogurt, honey, lime juice, sugar and a pinch of salt and process at high speed until smooth. Transfer to a bowl and refrigerate until needed. This will keep refrigerated in an airtight container for up to 3 days.

ROASTED PRAWNS Preheat the oven to 400°F. In a bowl, gently toss the prawns with 3 Tbsp of the olive oil and the cumin, salt and white pepper to taste until well coated.

Pour the remaining olive oil into a roasting pan along with the garlic and jalapeño and bake in the oven for 10 minutes, or until the garlic and pepper are mostly cooked and the oil is hot. Remove the pan from the oven, carefully add the prawns and immediately return to the oven for 3 to 4 minutes, or until the prawn shells begin to change colour. Use a spoon to quickly toss the prawns and cook them for a further 2 to 3 minutes. Remove from the oven and add the lemon juice and zest. Using a spoon, gently mix the lemon through the prawns.

TO SERVE Transfer the prawns to a serving platter and sprinkle with the cilantro. Pour the curry dressing into a dipping bowl and place it in the centre of the table so guests can serve themselves.

curry dressing

2 Tbsp grapeseed oil

2 cloves garlic, sliced

1-inch piece fresh ginger, peeled and thinly sliced

1 shallot, sliced

1½ Tbsp curry powder (we use a mild Madras)

1½ cups plain yogurt (do not use non-fat, as it can be watery)

6 tsp honey

Juice of 1 lime

1 tsp granulated sugar

Pinch of kosher or sea salt

roasted prawns

3 lb whole prawns or prawn tails, shells on

½ cup good-quality extra-virign olive oil, divided

1 tsp ground cumin

Sea salt and cracked white pepper to taste

2 cloves garlic, sliced

1 whole red jalapeño pepper, sliced, seeds removed

Juice and zest of 1 lemon

1 Tbsp chopped cilantro

FOR UNIQUE ITEMS, Araxi often looks to boutique market farmers who are tied to the land on smaller plots. Among them is the always-curious, sustainability-savvy Riley Johnson, whose picturesque Bandit Farms in the Pemberton Valley produces all manner of interesting edibles. In addition to Valley standards like carrots, peas, squash and brassicas, as well as uncommon items such as sunflower shoots, nettles and green tomatoes, Riley also conjures up nearly a dozen varieties of duck eggs year-round. From Indian Runners to Muscovys, Pekins and Khaki Campbells, chef James Walt uses them all in the restaurant to make fresh pasta. Though these specialty items are usually available only in small quantities, Chef Walt says: "There's a whole section of our inventory that includes delicious, seasonal one-offs and rarities. It's all amazing stuff, even if the invoice is written on the side of an old tomato box."

araxi | **GOING TO THE SOURCE**

Neon flying squid is a larger variety of squid found in British Columbia waters. It is sometimes under-utilized because of its size. Ask your local fishmonger to get it for you. Our salsify, a great root vegetable with a nutty, carroty flavour, comes from North Arm Farm in Pemberton. Together, these two ingredients make a really delicious combo. Before you begin this recipe, soak eight bamboo skewers, each six to eight inches long, in cold water for half an hour to prevent them from burning on the barbecue.

SERVES
4 FOR
LUNCH

grilled
neon squid
with salsify

Rinse the squid under cold running water and pat dry with paper towels. Using a sharp knife, score the squid in a ⅛-inch-deep crosshatch pattern on both sides. Next, cut the squid into 8 equal-sized strips and place in a bowl.

In a small bowl, combine the soy sauce, white wine and mirin (or honey) and whisk to combine. Pour this mixture over the squid and toss to coat. Refrigerate the squid while you prepare the salsify.

Pour the vegetable nage into a medium saucepan. Add the garlic, squeeze in the juice from the lemon halves and stir in the sugar and salt. Wash and peel the salsify, add it to the stock and cook on medium-low heat until it boils, 3 to 4 minutes. Turn down the heat to a simmer and cook, covered, for 15 to 20 minutes, or until the salsify is tender (check by cutting a small piece from the tip of the largest stalk and biting into it). Remove the pot from the heat and set it in a cool place.

Preheat the barbecue or an indoor grill on medium-high heat. Using a slotted spoon, transfer the salsify to a plate and cut it into 2-inch lengths. You will need 24 pieces. Remove the squid from the fridge. To assemble the skewers, thread the first 2 inches of a strip of squid onto the skewer, add a piece of salsify, then thread on 2 more inches of squid. Add another piece of salsify, 2 more inches of the squid, and a third piece of salsify. Repeat with the remaining squid and salsify until you have 8 skewers.

Brush the skewers with the leftover squid marinade, set them on the grill and cook for 2 minutes per side.

TO SERVE Place ¼ of the greens in the centre of each plate and top with 2 skewers of squid. Drizzle each serving with a spoonful of sesame-soy vinaigrette and sprinkle with parsley.

2 lb neon squid, body pieces (tentacles are a little chewy for this preparation)

¼ cup soy sauce

2 Tbsp dry white wine

2 Tbsp mirin or honey

4 cups Vegetable Nage (page 220)

2 cloves garlic

1 lemon, halved

1 Tbsp granulated sugar

1 tsp kosher or sea salt

8 large stalks salsify

3 cups mixed salad greens

½ cup Sesame-Soy Vinaigrette (page 219)

1 Tbsp chopped flat-leaf parsley

8 bamboo skewers, each 6 to 8 inches long

chilled poached salmon with cucumber & yogurt

POACHED SALMON Fill the bottom of a large fish-poaching pan about ⅔ full of water and bring to a light simmer on medium heat.

Measure the length of the salmon fillets. Cut a piece of plastic wrap at least 8 inches longer than the fillets and set it on a cutting board. Cut a second piece to the same size and set it on top of the first. Sprinkle about ½ of the chopped herbs down the centre of the plastic wrap, leaving about 4 inches uncovered at each end. Using your fingers, spread the herbs out to about the size of the fillets. Set one fillet, flesh side up, on top of the herbs. Using a pastry brush, brush the fish with all of the white wine. Sprinkle the gelatin as evenly as possible over the salmon, followed by the salt and white pepper.

Set the second fillet, flesh side down, on top of the first fillet. The thick end of one fillet should face the thin end of the other so that the 2 fillets together have a similar thickness all the way across. Sprinkle the remaining chopped herbs evenly over the fillet.

To wrap the salmon, fold the edge of the plastic wrap closest to you tightly over the salmon to create a log shape. Grasp the ends of the plastic wrap in each hand, gather them and continue rolling until the fish is completely enclosed. Twist the ends tightly to seal them and tie them securely with string or thick elastics to prevent them from coming open.

poached salmon

5 to 6 lb wild salmon, scaled, filleted and pin bones removed

1 cup chopped fresh soft-leaf herbs (e.g., parsley, chervil, tarragon) + 10 sprigs of the same herbs for garnish

1 Tbsp white wine

2 tsp powdered gelatin

2 tsp sea salt

1 tsp cracked white pepper

1 English cucumber, skin on, thinly sliced into rounds

Whole wild salmon is a real treat, and this is a good recipe to make it last for a few days or share with friends and family in your backyard. We like chinook or coho salmon for this recipe, as they have a slighter higher fat content than sockeye or pink. To make this dish, you will need a fish-poaching pan or another pan large and deep enough to hold the salmon; the other option is to cut the fillets in half and wrap and cook them separately. You will also need lots of plastic wrap and an accurate probe thermometer.

Using a probe thermometer, check the temperature of the water in the poaching pan. Adjust the heat until the thermometer reads 175°F. Carefully lower the wrapped salmon into the poaching pan and cook for 20 minutes (adjust the heat as needed to maintain this temperature).

Line a baking tray with several kitchen towels. As gently as possible, remove the wrapped salmon from the poaching liquid and transfer it to the tray to cool. Refrigerate the fish on the baking tray for at least 4 hours or (best) overnight.

CUCUMBER AND YOGURT Place the cucumber slices in a colander or fine-mesh sieve and sprinkle with the 1 Tbsp of salt. Let rest in the sink for at least 30 minutes to drain. At the same time, set a chinois or fine-mesh sieve over a bowl. Spoon the yogurt into the chinois (or sieve) and allow to drain for 30 minutes.

Transfer the drained cucumber and yogurt to a blender, add the garlic, olive oil, lemon juice and mint and purée at high speed until smooth. Season with salt and pepper. Season with more lemon juice if needed.

TO SERVE Remove the salmon from the fridge, leaving it wrapped for easier cutting, and place it on the cutting board. Using a sharp knife, cut the salmon into ½-inch slices, and peel away and discard the plastic wrap. Arrange the cucumber slices on a serving platter and top with the sliced salmon. Drizzle with a spoonful of the cucumber yogurt. Garnish with the fresh herbs.

cucumber and yogurt

2 large English cucumbers, peeled, seeds removed and cut into ½-inch rounds

1 Tbsp sea salt + more to taste

2 cups plain yogurt

2 cloves garlic, finely minced

2 Tbsp extra-virgin olive oil

Juice of 1 lemon

1 Tbsp finely chopped fresh mint

Ground black pepper to taste

CHILLED POACHED
SALMON WITH
CUCUMBER & YOGURT
page 60

STINGING NETTLE
GNOCCHI AND
KING CRAB
page 64

stinging nettle gnocchi & king crab

STINGING NETTLE GNOCCHI Fill a large bowl with ice water and have ready a clean dishtowel. Bring a large saucepan of lightly salted water to a boil on high heat. Using tongs or wearing gloves, add the nettles and cook for 30 seconds. Drain, refresh the nettles in the ice water and drain again. Place the nettles on the dishtowel, wrap the cloth around them and squeeze out any excess moisture. Transfer the dried nettles to a cutting board and chop them as finely as possible.

In a large bowl, combine the chopped nettles, ricotta, egg, salt and nutmeg until well mixed. Add the flour all at once, and using a fork or a pastry cutter, gently but swiftly work the mixture into a soft dough. Do not overwork the dough or the pasta will become tough. Lightly dust a large bowl, set the dough in it, cover with plastic wrap and let rise in the fridge for at least 30 minutes.

Lightly dust a clean work surface and a baking tray with flour. Place the dough on the counter and divide it into 4 even parts. Using your hands, roll each piece of dough into a rope ¾ inch in diameter. Using a small knife or a pastry scraper, cut the ropes into 1-inch lengths. (You will have roughly 50 pieces.) Arrange the individual gnocchi in a single layer on the baking tray and refrigerate, uncovered, until needed.

stinging nettle gnocchi

2 cups stinging nettles

1 lb ricotta, strained overnight in a fine-mesh sieve to remove moisture

1 whole large egg

1½ tsp kosher salt

¼ tsp fresh nutmeg

1 cup Italian "00" flour (see page 77)

Additional flour for dusting

Stinging nettles are abundant in the forests around Whistler and Pemberton in the spring and early summer. Look for them around the edges of your garden. They are very delicious and nutritious, but you need to be careful handling them in their raw state. Wear gloves until you have blanched or cooked them. You can make the gnocchi ahead of time without cooking them and refrigerate them for up to two days or freeze them for up to one month.

KING CRAB Heat the butter in a sauté pan on medium-low heat. Add the shallot and garlic and cook gently for 2 to 3 minutes, until softened and with a little colour. Stir in the mustard, cook for 1 to 2 minutes, then add the wine and cook until the liquid is evaporated, about 3 minutes. Pour in the cream and cook until reduced by half and lightly thickened, 3 to 4 minutes. Add the king crab meat and turn down the heat to low.

Finish gnocchi: Bring a large pot of salted water to a boil on high heat. Drop the gnocchi into the boiling water all at once and cook until most of them begin to float to the surface, 2 to 3 minutes. Using a slotted spoon, transfer the gnocchi to the pot of king crab. Gently toss to combine and remove from the heat.

TO SERVE Stir the chervil (or dill) and the chives into the gnocchi and sauce, then divide among 6 bowls and serve immediately.

king crab

¼ cup unsalted butter

1 large shallot, minced

2 cloves garlic, minced

1 Tbsp Dijon mustard

½ cup white wine

½ cup whipping cream

18 to 20 oz cooked king crab meat, removed from the shell in large (2 oz) pieces

1 Tbsp chopped chervil or dill

1 Tbsp finely chopped chives

CHORIZO-CRUSTED
LINGCOD WITH
TOMATO FONDUE
page 68

chorizo-crusted lingcod with tomato fondue

CHORIZO CRUST Cut 2 sheets of parchment paper, each 11 × 16 inches, and line a baking sheet with one of them. Set the second sheet aside.

In a small sauté pan, heat the olive oil on medium heat and sear the chorizo on each side for 3 minutes. Set aside to cool. Transfer the chorizo and the fat from the pan to a food processor, add the panko bread crumbs and purée for 2 minutes. Add the butter and process for another minute. Using a spatula, scrape the chorizo mixture onto the lined baking sheet, spreading it evenly, and cover with the second sheet of parchment. Using a rolling pin, roll out the crust to a thickness of ⅛ inch and refrigerate for 30 minutes to allow it to set.

TOMATO FONDUE Preheat the oven to 325°F. In an ovenproof saucepan fitted with a lid, heat the olive oil on medium-low heat. Add the onion and garlic and cook for 4 to 5 minutes, until the onion is softened and translucent and the garlic is fragrant. Stir in the tomato paste and cook for a further 3 minutes to bring out the flavour, then add the fresh tomatoes, thyme, rosemary, bay leaves and sugar. Season lightly with salt and mix thoroughly. Once the mixture comes to a simmer, cover and cook in the oven for about 40 minutes. Most of the juices should have cooked away and the tomatoes will have softened and thickened. Remove from the oven and set aside in a warm place until needed.

chorizo crust

2 Tbsp extra-virgin olive oil

10 oz cured chorizo, cut into ¼-inch slices

1 cup panko bread crumbs

¼ cup unsalted butter, softened and cut in small cubes

tomato fondue

¾ cup good-quality extra-virgin olive oil

1 white onion, finely chopped

5 cloves garlic, finely minced

3 Tbsp tomato paste

4 lb vine-ripened tomatoes, stems removed, coarsely chopped

3 sprigs thyme

Sprig of rosemary

2 bay leaves

2 Tbsp granulated sugar

Sea salt to taste

Chefs love lingcod. Not only is this sustainable local fish extremely flavourful, but it is also very moist, takes on other flavours well and is much more affordable than other white fish such as sablefish and halibut. Try the chorizo crust with chicken or as the top layer on your lasagna.

LINGCOD Preheat the oven to 400°F. Line a baking tray with parchment paper. Using a pastry brush, brush the lingcod fillets with the olive oil and place them on the baking tray. Lightly season with sea salt. Remove the chorizo crust from the fridge. Using a sharp knife, cut 6 rectangles that cover the lingcod fillets as much as possible. Place the crusts over the fish and bake for 8 minutes. Rotate the tray 180 degrees and cook for 4 more minutes. The fish should be firm to the touch, the crust lightly brown. A sharp knife inserted into the centre of the thickest fillet should come out warm.

TO SERVE Place a spoonful of the tomato fondue in the centre of each plate. Place a chorizo-crusted lingcod fillet on top and garnish with sprigs of chervil (or parsley).

lingcod

6 line-caught skinless, boneless lingcod fillets, each 7 oz

1 Tbsp good-quality extra-virgin olive oil

Pinch of sea salt

12 sprigs chervil or flat-leaf parsley

flaked lingcod "chowder" with broccoli

MUSSEL BROTH Have ready a large bowl. In a medium saucepan fitted with a lid, heat the olive oil on medium heat. Add the shallots and cook until just softened, 2 to 3 minutes. Add the mussels, thyme and bay leaves and heat for 1 minute. Pour in the wine and immediately cover with the lid to steam the mussels. Remove the lid after 2 minutes and transfer the mussels from the broth to the bowl as they open. If any of the mussels have not opened within a further 2 minutes, discard them. Remove the pot from the heat.

Place a fine-mesh sieve over a clean bowl and strain the leftover broth from the pot. Discard the solids.

Once the mussels have cooled enough to handle, remove the meat from the shells. Discard the shells. Set aside the mussel meat and the stock to make the chowder.

MUSSEL CHOWDER In a medium saucepan on low heat, gently heat the fish (or vegetable) stock, mussel broth, milk and bay leaf. In a second medium saucepan, melt the butter on medium heat. Slowly add the flour, whisking gently to form a roux. Turn down the heat to low and cook for 5 minutes. Whisk in the hot broth–milk mixture, slowly at first to avoid lumps. Gently simmer this velouté sauce for 10 minutes, then stir in the cream. Set a fine-mesh sieve over a clean bowl, strain the sauce through it and set aside. Discard the solids.

Heat the grapeseed oil in a medium saucepan on medium heat. Add the bacon and sauté until lightly crisped, about 5 minutes. Stir in the potato, leek and carrot and sauté for 3 to 4 minutes. Pour off any excess oil, then stir in the celery and the velouté sauce and simmer until the potato is tender, 8 to 10 minutes. Add the mussel meat to warm it through.

mussel broth

1 Tbsp extra-virgin olive oil

2 shallots, thinly sliced

2 lb mussels, beards removed, rinsed

Sprig of thyme

2 bay leaves

¾ cup white wine

mussel chowder

2 cups fish or vegetable stock

1 cup mussel broth

1 cup whole milk

1 bay leaf

¼ cup unsalted butter

¼ cup all-purpose flour, sifted

¼ cup whipping cream

1 Tbsp grapeseed oil

2 slices bacon, diced

1 large Yukon Gold or Kennebec potato, peeled and diced

1 medium leek, white and light green parts only, sliced and rinsed

1 medium carrot, diced

2 stalks celery, diced

Reserved mussel meat

1 Tbsp chopped flat-leaf parsley

This delicious chowder is a great stand-alone soup, and though it has several steps, none of them is difficult. We like to use Pacific Golden Mussels from Quadra or Saltspring Island, but you can substitute halibut for the lingcod or look for local rockfish, which is a real treat as well. For best results, bring the chowder to a light simmer while you sauté the broccoli.

LINGCOD Preheat the oven to 375°F. Fill a large bowl with ice water.

Bring a medium saucepan of lightly salted water to a boil on high heat. Add the broccoli and cook for 2 minutes. Using a slotted spoon, transfer the broccoli to the ice water to stop the cooking. Discard the cooking water. Once the broccoli has cooled, drain and set aside.

Place the lingcod fillet in a shallow ovenproof dish, drizzle with 1 Tbsp of the olive oil and season with salt. Sprinkle the lemon juice and zest evenly over the lingcod, then bake, uncovered, for 10 minutes. Remove the dish from the oven and, using a spoon, baste the lingcod with the cooking juices. Return to the oven and cook for a further 6 to 8 minutes, then remove from the oven and let stand in a warm place. Baste the lingcod a few more times. The fish should be flaky and moist.

In a sauté pan, heat the remaining 2 Tbsp of olive oil on medium heat. Once hot, add the garlic and cook until lightly golden, 2 to 3 minutes. Stir in the broccoli and toss to coat with the olive oil and garlic. Add a pinch of chilies, season with salt and cook for 2 minutes, until thoroughly heated. Remove from the heat.

TO SERVE Bring the mussel chowder to a simmer on low heat, add the chopped parsley and ladle into individual bowls. Using a fork, flake off pieces of the lingcod and divide them evenly among the bowls, placing them on the chowder. Top with the sautéed broccoli and drizzle with olive oil and garlic from the pan. Serve hot.

lingcod

2 large heads organic broccoli, cut into florets

2 to 3 lb skinless, boneless lingcod fillet

3 Tbsp extra-virgin olive oil

Pinch of sea salt

Juice and zest of 1 lemon

2 cloves garlic, sliced

Pinch of dried red chilies

spot prawn, corn & herb risotto

Using a sharp knife, cut the corn kernels off the cobs. (An easy way to do this is to slice the cob once to square the edge and then rotate the cob, slicing off the remaining kernels.) Reserve the cobs and place the kernels in a bowl.

In a stockpot on medium-low heat, melt 2 Tbsp of the butter with 1 Tbsp of the olive oil. Stir in the sliced onion and cook until softened and translucent, 5 to 6 minutes. Add all of the corn cobs and mix to coat with butter and onion slices. Cover the cobs with water and increase the heat to high. When the water reaches a boil, turn down the heat to a simmer and cook the cobs for 10 minutes. Remove from the heat and let stand for a further 10 minutes. Set a fine-mesh sieve over a clean, medium pot and strain the corn stock through it. You should have about 5 cups. Discard the cobs.

Fill a large bowl with ice water. Bring some lightly salted water to a boil in a large stockpot on high heat. Add the corn kernels and cook for 3 minutes to soften them. Using a slotted spoon, transfer the corn to the bowl of ice water to stop the cooking. Drain and set aside 1½ cups of kernels. Reserve the rest in an airtight container in the fridge for salads or other dishes.

To cook the risotto, bring the corn stock to a simmer on low heat and then turn off the heat.

8 ears of fresh corn, husks removed

6 Tbsp unsalted butter

3 Tbsp extra-virgin olive oil

2 medium white onions: 1 sliced, 1 minced

Sea salt to taste

3 cups arborio rice

½ cup white wine

1 lb spot prawn tails, peeled and deveined

¾ cup grated Parmesan cheese

1 Tbsp chopped flat-leaf parsley

1 Tbsp chopped fresh chervil

1 Tbsp chopped fresh chives

Juice and zest of 1 lemon

Fresh herb leaves, for garnish

Of all the dishes we serve in the restaurant, I think this is the one for which we get the most recipe requests. So here it is! Enjoy.

Heat the remaining 2 Tbsp of olive oil in a large saucepan on medium heat and then add the minced onion. Season lightly with salt and cook until softened and translucent, about 4 minutes. Add all of the rice, mixing thoroughly, and cook for about 3 minutes. Deglaze the pot with the wine and cook for about 3 minutes, until the wine has been absorbed. Season lightly with more salt.

Ladle about 1 cup of the corn stock into the pot of rice and stir gently until it is all absorbed, 4 to 5 minutes. Add another cup of stock and stir again until the stock is absorbed, 4 to 5 minutes. Repeat twice more, adding 1 cup at a time and waiting until it has been absorbed. At this point, the rice is close to being cooked. Stir in the corn and about ½ cup of the corn stock and mix gently, then add the spot prawns and very gently stir in an additional ½ cup of the stock. Be careful not to break up the prawns too much.

Once the prawns have turned a light pink and firmed up, about 3 minutes, remove the pot from the heat. Add the remaining 4 Tbsp of butter, all of the cheese and blend gently. Once the butter and cheese are incorporated, add a little salt if needed. Gently stir in the parsley, chervil, chives and the lemon juice and zest. Mix well and, while still very hot, pour the risotto into a large serving bowl and garnish with herb leaves.

duck egg pasta tortellini with duck confit filling

DUCK CONFIT FILLING Heat the grapeseed (or vegetable) oil in a large sauté pan on medium heat. Add the shiitake mushrooms and sauté for 2 to 3 minutes, until lightly golden. Stir in the shredded duck meat and cook for 2 minutes more, then add the ginger and sauté for 2 minutes. Add the hoisin and oyster sauces and season lightly with salt and pepper. Remove from the heat and mix in the green onions. Transfer the duck to a bowl, cover and refrigerate until well chilled, about 1 hour.

FRESH DUCK EGG PASTA DOUGH Combine the duck eggs, duck egg yolks and olive oil in a large bowl and mix gently with a fork to break the yolks. Place the flour and salt in a food processor and blend for 10 seconds to aerate. With the machine running, slowly pour in the egg mixture and process just until combined.

Turn the dough out onto a clean work surface. Bring the dough together with your hands and knead for 5 to 7 minutes, until it is smooth. Wrap the dough in plastic wrap and let it rest for 30 minutes before using. Tightly wrapped, it will keep refrigerated for up to 2 days.

To prepare the pasta, have ready a 4-inch round cookie cutter or glass. Lightly moisten a clean dishtowel with cold water. Following the instructions on your pasta machine, divide the dough into 2 equal parts and roll out each one into a sheet the thickness of a dime. Using the cookie cutter or the glass, cut each piece of dough into 24 rounds for a total of 48 rounds. Arrange the rounds in a single stack and cover them with the damp cloth.

Lightly dust a baking sheet with flour and fill a small bowl with water. Fill a large roasting pan with ice. Place the bowl of duck filling on the ice while you work with the dough.

duck confit filling

2 Tbsp grapeseed or vegetable oil

2 packed cups shiitake mushrooms, stems removed and caps sliced

4 pieces duck leg confit, skin and bones removed and meat shredded (about 1½ cups of meat)

1 Tbsp minced fresh ginger

2 Tbsp hoisin sauce

1 Tbsp oyster sauce

Sea salt and ground black pepper to taste

¼ cup chopped green onions, both white and green parts

fresh duck egg pasta dough

7 oz duck eggs (about 2 large)

4 oz duck egg yolks (about 3 large)

1 Tbsp extra-virgin olive oil

4 cups Italian "00" flour (see opposite)

1 tsp kosher or sea salt

1 egg lightly beaten with 2 Tbsp cold water

The "OO" flour is durum wheat flour that works very well for pasta and gnocchi. It is readily available in grocery stores, but you can also substitute all-purpose flour. If you have never had a duck egg, you have to try one; they are rich and delicious. And you can make your own duck confit (see the great recipe in our first cookbook, *Araxi: Seasonal Recipes from the Celebrated Whistler Restaurant*). We use duck legs from Yarrow Meadows and duck eggs from Bandit Farms.

Place one pasta round on a clean work surface. Spoon 2 tsp of the filling onto the centre of the pasta, then, using a pastry brush, lightly brush the edges of the round with water. Fold the top half of the pasta over the bottom half to form a semi-circle, being careful to completely enclose the filling. Press the edges tightly from the centre to the outer edge to force out any air and create a tight seal. Place this semi-circle of pasta, with the flat edge towards you, across the middle of your index finger. Be sure there is an even amount of pasta on both sides of your finger. Dab a small amount of water on one corner of the semi-circle, then fold the pasta around your finger, bringing the two tips together. With the thumb and forefinger of your other hand, press the tips together tightly to seal, then carefully slide this tortellini off your finger. Place this finished tortellini on the baking sheet, and continue filling and shaping the remaining tortellini until you have used up all the pasta and the filling. Set aside the pasta while you prepare the glaze.

Any leftover filling can be frozen in an airtight container for up to 2 weeks.

FINISHING GLAZE Bring a large saucepan of salted water to a boil on high heat.

In a small saucepan, combine the vegetable nage and soy sauce and bring to a boil on high heat. Turn down the heat and whisk in the cold butter, a few cubes at a time, until emulsified. Add the chives, remove from the heat and set aside in a warm place.

Add the tortellini to the pot of boiling water and cook for 4 to 5 minutes. Using a slotted spoon, transfer the cooked pasta to a large platter or bowl. Drizzle the tortellini with the glaze, tossing gently to coat well, then sprinkle with the Parmesan cheese and serve immediately.

finishing glaze
½ cup Vegetable Nage (page 220)
2 Tbsp soy sauce
¼ cup unsalted butter, cold, cut into ¼-inch cubes
2 Tbsp chopped fresh chives
2 oz grated Parmesan cheese

DUCK EGG PASTA
TORTELLINI WITH
DUCK CONFIT FILLING
page 76

pork jowls with asparagus & peas

Rinse the pork jowls under cold running water and pat them dry with paper towels. Place the pork in a large bowl and completely cover it with the duck brine. Cover and refrigerate for 24 hours.

Preheat the oven to 325°c. Remove the jowls from the brine, pat them dry, then place them in a medium ovenproof saucepan fitted with an ovenproof lid. Add the onion, carrot and celery and the vegetable nage, and bring to a simmer on medium heat. Remove from the heat, cover with the lid and place in the oven for 2½ hours, or until soft and very tender. Remove from the oven and set aside, still covered.

Line a 9 × 5-inch loaf pan or terrine mould with plastic wrap. Using a slotted spoon, transfer the jowls to a clean work surface. Use a spoon to scrape off and discard any excess fat, then place a jowl in the loaf pan (or terrine mould). Sprinkle with a little salt. Repeat the layering of meat and salt until you have used all the jowls, then tightly cover the pan (or mould) with plastic wrap. Set a second pan of similar size (or slightly smaller) on top of the jowls and place a little weight, such as a 28 oz can, on it. Refrigerate the pan overnight to press the jowls.

To cook the jowls, unwrap the meat, discarding the plastic wrap, and slice the jowls into 2-inch pieces. Transfer them to a plate.

4 lb pork jowls

4 cups Duck Brine (page 186)

1 onion, cut into quarters

1 large carrot, peeled and cut into quarters

2 stalks celery, cut into quarters

6 cups Vegetable Nage (page 220)

Sea salt to taste

24 asparagus spears, fibrous stems trimmed

2 cups fresh, shelled peas

2 Tbsp unsalted butter

1 tsp sea salt

½ tsp curry powder (we use a mild Madras)

2 Tbsp extra-virgin olive oil

5 sprigs herb leaves (chervil, flat-leaf parsley, fennel or dill) for garnish

Pork jowls, not to be confused with pork cheeks, are the cut that butchers use to make the famous Italian cured meat guanciale. Ask your local butcher to acquire them for you. It's best to prepare this dish a couple of days before you plan to serve it, as the pork needs time to marinate and be pressed. This dish is well worth the time and effort, believe me, and makes enough to feed a couple of extra friends.

Preheat the oven to 200°F to keep the jowls warm. Heat a nonstick sauté pan on medium heat. Once hot, add the meat slices, in batches if necessary (do not overcrowd the pan), and cook for 2 minutes. Use tongs to turn them gently as they will have become quite soft and golden brown. Cook for 2 more minutes, then transfer to a clean plate and keep warm in the oven.

Bring a medium saucepan of lightly salted water to a boil on high heat. Drop the asparagus spears into the water, cook for 90 seconds and, using a slotted spoon, transfer them to a serving bowl. Immediately drop the peas into the same boiling water and cook for 2 minutes. Use the slotted spoon to transfer the peas to the same bowl as the asparagus. While still hot, stir in the butter, salt and curry powder and toss gently to coat the veggies.

TO SERVE Arrange the asparagus and peas on a serving platter and top them with the sliced jowls. Drizzle with olive oil and garnish with fresh herb leaves.

romy's chicken under the brick

ROMY'S CHICKEN Preheat the oven to 425°F. Rinse the chicken inside and out under cold running water and pat dry with paper towels. Using a sharp knife, make an incision 2 inches long down the thigh and drumstick of each leg. This step allows the thighs and legs to cook evenly with the breasts.

In a small bowl, combine the mustard and 1 Tbsp of the vegetable oil. Using a pastry brush, evenly cover the skin with this mixture, then sprinkle the chicken with the panko, covering the skin completely. Use your hands to gently press the bread crumbs into the chicken so they adhere. Shake off any excess.

Heat the remaining 3 Tbsp of vegetable oil in a large ovenproof skillet on medium heat. Place the chicken, breaded side down, in the pan and sear it for 1 minute. Set the brick on top of the chicken and bake in the oven for 10 to 12 minutes. Remove the skillet from the oven, carefully remove and set aside the brick, turn the chicken over and return to the oven for a further 10 minutes. To check the chicken for doneness, insert a knife into the thickest part of the leg. The juices should run clear and the tip of the knife should be hot. Remove the chicken from the oven and set it aside to rest while you prepare the shallots.

romy's chicken

1 large free-range chicken, about 4 lb, split in half and backbone removed

3 Tbsp Dijon mustard

4 Tbsp vegetable oil

1 cup panko bread crumbs

Sea salt and ground black pepper to taste

1 standard building brick, wrapped with foil

Romy Prasad is not only a great chef but also a great friend. We were classmates at the Stratford Chefs School, way back… I don't want to say when. My wife and I thoroughly enjoyed this dish when Romy was cooking at CinCin Ristorante in Vancouver; it's just a great way to cook chicken. Use a nice brick from your backyard or buy one at any home-building centre, or use a heavy cast-iron pan instead.

ROSEMARY-ROASTED SHALLOTS Preheat the oven to 350°F. Heat the butter and oil in a large ovenproof sauté pan on medium-high heat. Add the shallots and cook until they start to caramelize slightly, 3 to 4 minutes. Stir in the rosemary and bake in the oven for 15 minutes. The shallots should be golden and soft. Set aside in a warm place until needed.

TARRAGON SALSA Place the bread, garlic, tarragon leaves and tarragon vinegar in a food processor or blender and purée at medium speed. With the motor running, slowly add the olive oil in a thin, continuous stream until the salsa reaches a smooth consistency. Season with a pinch of salt, transfer to a small bowl and refrigerate until needed.

TO SERVE Set the chicken on a clean cutting board. Separate the chicken into two halves by splitting it down the breast bone with a sharp knife. Cut each breast in half and separate out the drumstick and thighs. (You should have 8 pieces of chicken: 4 pieces of breast meat, 2 thighs and 2 drumsticks.) Arrange the shallots on a serving platter, top with the chicken and drizzle with the tarragon salsa.

rosemary-roasted shallots

3 Tbsp unsalted butter

1 tsp vegetable oil

18 medium shallots, peeled

4 sprigs rosemary

tarragon salsa

2 slices day-old bread, cut into cubes

1 clove garlic, sliced

½ cup fresh tarragon leaves

2 Tbsp tarragon vinegar

¼ cup extra-virgin olive oil

Pinch of kosher or sea salt

araxi | GOING TO THE SOURCE

ARAXI HAS BEEN buying arugula, carrots, peas, carrots, kale, radishes, beans, chard, spinach, tomatoes and much more from Simone MacIsaac and Sarah McMillan since they launched Rootdown Organic Farm in 2009. The sprawling Pemberton Meadows property is perfectly situated on the rich soils between glacial Ryan Creek and the mighty Lillooet River. The mountainous surroundings couldn't be more different from where Sarah grew up in Australia. Like many young expats from Oz, she was initially drawn to Whistler's easygoing lifestyle (it's the stuff of legend in Australia) but soon saw beyond it to fall for the land itself. Sarah actually worked at Araxi as a bartender before she became a farmer. The restaurant has supported her from the start, and her spicy mustard greens have become the stuff of local legend. Each spring the restaurant zeroes in on Rootdown's green and red tatsoi, arugula, mizuna and ruby streaks to augment its salads. Many Araxi staff members also buy into her popular CSA (community-supported agriculture) program, which brings fresh produce to their home kitchens every month.

SPICED LAMB
MEATBALLS
"BAR OSO"
page 86

SERVES
4 TO 6
AS PART
OF AN
ENTRÉE
PLATTER

spiced lamb meatballs "bar oso"

TOMATO SAUCE Heat the olive oil in a large saucepan on medium heat. Add the onion and garlic and cook until softened, 7 to 8 minutes. Pour in the canned tomatoes and juice, breaking them up with a wooden spoon, then add the tomato paste and basil. Stir well, add the sugar and salt and cook for 20 minutes. Remove from the heat.

Carefully transfer the tomato mixture to a blender and purée at high speed until smooth. Set a coarse sieve over a clean bowl and strain the tomato sauce through it. Discard the solids. Set the sauce aside while you prepare the meatballs.

MEATBALLS Heat the olive oil in a sauté pan on medium heat. Add the onion and garlic, season with some of the sea salt and cook until the onion is softened and translucent, 3 to 4 minutes. Remove from the heat and scrape the onion and garlic into a bowl.

In a small bowl, mix the milk with the bread crumbs to form a paste.

In a large bowl, mix the lamb with the cooked onion, bread crumb mixture and eggs until well combined. Add the salt, pepper, paprika, nutmeg, and cumin along with the Parmesan cheese and parsley. Using your hands, thoroughly mix these ingredients together. Refrigerate the meat mixture for 30 minutes.

tomato sauce

¾ cup extra-virgin olive oil

1 medium onion, minced

3 cloves garlic, minced

3 cans (each 28 fl oz) peeled tomatoes, juice reserved

3 Tbsp tomato paste

1 cup fresh basil, stems and leaves

1 Tbsp granulated sugar

1 Tbsp kosher or sea salt

fresh herbs, for garnish

meatballs

2 Tbsp extra-virgin olive oil

1 medium white onion, minced

4 cloves garlic, minced

¾ cup whole milk

¾ cup bread crumbs (fresh or dried)

3 lb ground lamb (leg or shoulder)

2 eggs, lightly beaten

1½ Tbsp sea salt

1 tsp cracked black pepper

1 tsp smoked paprika

½ tsp ground nutmeg

1 tsp ground cumin

1 cup grated Parmesan cheese

3 Tbsp chopped flat-leaf parsley

2 Tbsp grapeseed oil

This is a recipe we developed for our newest venture, Bar Oso, which features Spanish-inspired small plates. *Oso* means "bear" in Spanish, and Bar Oso's name salutes the lovely animals we share Whistler with. For this recipe, use the best local lamb you can find—it is always out there. And once the meatballs have been cooked in the sauce, refrigerate them for two to three days, as their flavour only gets better with time.

Fill a bowl with water. Moisten your hands slightly with the water to prevent the meat from sticking, then, using a large soup spoon or a small ice cream scoop and your hands, shape the meat mixture into twenty-four 2 oz balls. Arrange the meatballs on a plate and refrigerate for at least 30 minutes, and up to 24 hours. They should be covered if being refrigerated for more than an hour.

Preheat the oven to 325°F. Heat the grapeseed oil in a large sauté pan on medium heat. Place the meatballs in the pan, working in batches if necessary (do not crowd the pan), and brown on all sides, 2 to 3 minutes total. Transfer the browned meatballs to a casserole dish fitted with a lid. (Repeat with the remaining meatballs if you are cooking them in batches.)

Gently reheat the tomato sauce on medium-low heat, then cover the meatballs with the warm tomato sauce. Cover with the lid, place the casserole dish in the centre of the oven and cook for 30 minutes. Remove the dish from the oven, turn the meatballs over, cover again and cook for a further 15 minutes.

TO SERVE Spoon the meatballs onto a serving platter. Using a spoon, skim off and discard any fatty juices from the top of the sauce. Spoon the sauce over the meatballs and garnish with fresh herbs.

lavender meringues with blueberries & mint

MERINGUES Set the racks in the upper and lower thirds of the oven and preheat the oven to 250°F. Line 2 large baking trays with parchment paper and have ready a stainless steel bowl that fits over a medium saucepan.

Fill the saucepan ¼ full with water and bring to a simmer on medium heat. Crack the egg whites into the metal bowl and set it over the saucepan. Swirl the egg whites in the bowl until barely warm to the touch, about 3 minutes, then pour them into the bowl of a stand mixer fitted with the whisk attachment. Add the salt and beat at high speed until the egg whites hold soft peaks, 4 to 5 minutes.

Turn down the speed to low, gradually add 1½ cups of the sugar, then increase the speed to medium-high and beat until the meringue holds stiff, glossy peaks, 4 to 5 minutes.

In a small bowl, stir together the remaining ¼ cup of sugar, the cornstarch and the lavender. With the mixer running at low speed, add this mixture to the meringue and process until well incorporated. Fold in the vinegar.

Spoon 4 mounds of meringue, each about 2 inches high and about ½ cup in volume, onto each lined baking tray, leaving about 1 inch around each one. Place the baking trays in the oven and cook the meringues for about 30 minutes. Switch the position of

meringues

8 egg whites

⅛ tsp sea salt

1¾ cups granulated sugar

1 Tbsp cornstarch

2 tsp dried lavender, slightly crushed

1 Tbsp berry vinegar (any flavour)

2 cups whipped cream, for garnish

1 cup fresh blueberries, for garnish

8 mint leaves, for garnish

When used sparingly, lavender is a great flavour. Too much of it, however, tastes like soap. We use only a small amount of dried lavender for this recipe. You can find it in the spice section at fine grocers or at farmers' markets or, in season, you can pick some fresh from your garden, hang it upside down in a dry place for a few weeks and use that. I always love fresh blueberries, but cooked blueberries pair beautifully with the meringue.

the baking trays (moving the tray on the upper rack to the lower and vice versa) and bake for another 30 to 45 minutes, until the meringues are crisp but still soft inside. If the meringues are still not crisp after 1¼ hours, turn off the oven and allow them to cool inside for 30 minutes.

Once the meringues are cool enough to touch, transfer them from the parchment paper to wire racks to cool. (They may stick if cooled completely on the parchment paper.)

BLUEBERRY COMPOTE Combine all of the ingredients in a small saucepan and bring to a boil on medium-high heat. Stir constantly to ensure the berries do not burn. Turn down the heat to a simmer and cook for about 5 minutes, until the blueberries just start to break down. Remove from the heat, transfer to a bowl and refrigerate immediately until cool. Remove and discard the vanilla bean pod.

TO SERVE Arrange the meringues on individual plates or on a large serving platter. Spoon a generous amount of berry compote into the centre of each one and then top with a spoonful of whipped cream. Garnish with fresh blueberries on and around the meringues and top with a mint leaf (or two).

blueberry compote

3 cups fresh blueberries

¼ cup granulated sugar

½ tsp fresh lemon juice

½ vanilla bean, cut lengthwise and seeds scraped

These soft chocolatey cookies are perfect served warm with a glass of cold milk. They are best on the day they are baked, but if you can't find enough family and friends to eat all four dozen at once, make the dough, roll it into logs and freeze. Then, when you have a craving for something sweet, remove the dough from the freezer, slice off a few pieces and bake them for a nice warm treat.

MAKES
4 DOZEN
COOKIES

triple chocolate cookies

Have ready a stainless steel bowl that fits over a medium saucepan. Fill the saucepan ¼ full with water and bring to a simmer on medium heat. Place the 64% and 55% dark chocolates and the butter in the bowl and set it over the water, stirring until the ingredients are melted together. Remove from the heat and set aside.

Place the eggs and granulated sugar in the bowl of a stand mixer fitted with the whisk attachment and process at high speed until light and fluffy, 8 to 10 minutes. Using a spatula, fold in the espresso and vanilla. Fold the egg mixture into the warm chocolate mixture.

In a small bowl, combine the flour, baking powder and salt with the chocolate chips, white chocolate and walnuts. Add to the chocolate-egg mixture and mix by hand until just combined. Refrigerate the dough until firm enough to handle, about 1 hour.

Lightly dust a clean work surface with the icing sugar. Divide the dough into 4 equal parts and, using your hands, roll each piece into a log 12 inches long and about 1½ inches in diameter. Roll each log in the icing sugar to prevent it from sticking. Set the logs on a plate and refrigerate, uncovered, until firm, about 30 minutes.

Preheat the oven to 325°F. Line a baking tray with parchment paper. Using a sharp knife, cut each log into 12 to 14 equal slices and place them, cut side down, on the lined baking tray. Place the first baking tray on a second one so the cookies bake evenly and the bottoms do not burn. Bake for 10 minutes, until the edges of the cookies are just set and the centres are still soft. Do not overbake.

Transfer the cookies to a wire rack to cool slightly, but serve warm. Leftovers will keep in an airtight container at room temperature for 2 to 3 days.

3 oz dark chocolate (64% cocoa)

8 oz dark chocolate (55% cocoa)

4 Tbsp unsalted butter

2 large eggs, at room temperature

¾ cup + 1 Tbsp granulated sugar

1 tsp chilled espresso coffee

½ tsp pure vanilla extract

¾ cup + 1 Tbsp all-purpose flour

1 tsp baking powder

¼ tsp kosher or sea salt

4 oz dark chocolate chips (¾ cup)

4 oz coarsely chopped white chocolate (¾ cup)

¾ cup chopped walnuts

¾ cup icing sugar (for dusting)

Buttermilk gives this panna cotta a nice tangy flavour that works really well with the strawberries. Ours usually come still warm from the sun at North Arm Farm in Pemberton. Look for vanilla sugar in the bakery section of your supermarket, or make your own by scraping a fresh vanilla bean and adding the seeds and pod to three cups of granulated sugar and letting the mixture stand in an airtight container for a week or two.

buttermilk panna cotta with strawberries

Have ready eight 4 oz ramekins or dessert glasses and a large bowl full of ice. In a small bowl, soak the gelatin in enough cold water to cover until soft, about 5 minutes.

Combine the cream, vanilla bean and sugar in a small saucepan and bring to a boil on high heat. Remove the hot cream mixture from the heat and transfer it to a bowl. Using your hands, squeeze the excess water from the gelatin and add it to the hot cream mixture. Stir until completely dissolved, then pour in the buttermilk and stir to incorporate.

Set a fine chinois or a fine-mesh sieve over a medium stainless steel bowl and strain the cream mixture through it. Discard the solids. Set the bowl of hot cream over the bowl of ice. Whisk constantly until the panna cotta starts to thicken slightly to ensure that no lumps form. Immediately pour the mixture into the ramekins (or glasses) and chill, uncovered, until set, at least 4 hours or (best) overnight.

In a bowl, combine the strawberries, simple syrup and pepper and toss well to coat. Spoon equal amounts of the strawberry mixture over each chilled panna cotta and serve immediately.

6 sheets gelatin

3 cups whipping cream

1 vanilla bean, cut lengthwise and seeds scraped out

½ cup granulated sugar or vanilla-infused sugar

1½ cups buttermilk

2 cups fresh local strawberries, washed and cut in half

2 Tbsp Simple Syrup (page 219)

½ tsp cracked black pepper

cherry ice cream bars

MACERATED CHERRIES Place the cherries, simple syrup, brandy, lemon juice and vanilla bean in a 4-cup airtight container, seal tightly and allow to macerate overnight.

VANILLA ICE CREAM Combine the cream, milk and vanilla in a medium saucepan and bring to a boil on medium-high heat. Remove from the heat, cover tightly with a lid and let infuse for 10 minutes. Strain the mixture through a fine-mesh sieve into a large clean saucepan. Discard the vanilla bean pod.

Fill a large bowl with ice. Return the infused cream to medium-high heat and bring just to a boil. In a large bowl, whisk together the egg yolks with the sugar until light and creamy. Gently pour the boiled cream over the yolks and sugar, whisking constantly, then return the entire mixture to the pot. Cook on medium heat, stirring constantly with a heatproof spatula, until the mixture thickens enough to coat the back of the spatula. Remove from the heat. While still warm, strain the cream mixture through a fine-mesh sieve into a clean bowl. Set the bowl with the cream mixture over the bowl of ice and refrigerate for at least 4 hours, or (best) overnight.

Once chilled, scrape the vanilla ice cream base into an ice cream maker and churn according to the manufacturer's instructions. Keep frozen for up to a week until ready to build the ice cream bars.

FLOURLESS CHOCOLATE CAKE Preheat the oven to 375°F. Lightly grease an 11 × 18-inch pan and line it with parchment paper.

Combine the egg yolks, cream and cocoa powder in the bowl of a stand mixer fitted with the paddle attachment. Mix at the lowest speed until the ingredients just come together, about 3 minutes. Increase the speed to medium and process until you have a smooth cocoa paste, 2 to 3 minutes. Transfer this paste to a large clean bowl and set aside.

macerated cherries

2 cups pitted Okanagan cherries

2 cups Simple Syrup (page 219)

½ cup brandy

Juice of 1 lemon

½ vanilla bean, split lengthwise and seeds scraped

vanilla ice cream

2 cups whipping cream

¾ cup whole milk

½ vanilla bean, split lengthwise and seeds scraped

½ cup + 1 Tbsp granulated sugar

8 egg yolks

flourless chocolate cake

6 egg yolks

¾ cup whipping cream

¼ cup cocoa powder, sifted

7 egg whites

¾ cup + 1 Tbsp granulated sugar

chocolate "dip" mixture

18 oz dark chocolate (60 to 70% cocoa)

4 oz cocoa butter (available at fine grocers or ask at your local pastry shop)

2 dozen fresh cherries, washed and stemmed, for garnish

Give yourself plenty of time to make these ice cream bars. They are not difficult but there are a few steps: the cherries need at least twelve hours to macerate, the ice cream takes a few hours to chill and, once assembled, the layers take at least six hours to freeze before you can cut them into bars. If necessary, you can make them ahead and keep them frozen in an airtight container for up to a month. The end result is well worth the effort.

Thoroughly wash and dry the mixing bowl and fit the mixer with a whisk attachment. Place the egg whites and sugar in the bowl and whisk on medium speed until the sugar is roughly distributed. Increase to the highest speed and whisk the mixture until it forms soft peaks, about 6 minutes.

Using a spatula, fold ⅓ of this meringue into the cocoa paste and mix until smooth. Gently fold in the remaining meringue and mix until fully combined. Scrape the cake batter into the pan, using a palette knife to smooth the surface. Bake for 10 minutes, then rotate the cake pan 180 degrees to ensure even cooking and bake for about 5 minutes more, or until the cake springs back when pressed but is still moist. Transfer the pan to a wire rack.

Cut a piece of parchment paper larger than the size of the pan. Place a knife between the edge of the pan and the cake to loosen it. Invert the cake onto the parchment. Remove the pan, then carefully flip the cake, with the original parchment still attached, back onto the cooling rack. Set aside to cool completely.

TO ASSEMBLE Line the sides and bottom of a 9-inch square cake pan with parchment paper. Remove the ice cream from the freezer and let it soften slightly in the fridge.

Remove and discard the parchment paper from the cooled flourless cake and set it on a clean work surface. Cut the cake in half along the 18-inch side to create two 9-inch wide cakes. Trim the 11-inch side of both cakes to fit into the prepared cake pan. Place one cake in the pan and set the other one aside.

Remove the ice cream from the fridge and transfer it to a large bowl. Using a rubber spatula, soften it enough that it reaches a spreadable consistency.

Drain the syrup from the macerated cherries into a small jar and reserve it for another use. Using the rubber spatula, fold the cherries into the ice cream and mix thoroughly. Spread all of the cherry ice cream evenly over the cake in the pan. *continued overleaf*

Place the second 9-inch cake on top of the ice cream and press down gently to make the layer as even as possible. Cover with plastic wrap and place in the freezer for at least 4 to 6 hours, until well frozen.

Once the cake is well frozen, remove it from the freezer and set it on a clean work surface. Have ready a bowl of hot water, a serrated knife, a ruler and a kitchen towel. You will be cutting the cake into twelve $4\frac{1}{2} \times 1\frac{1}{2}$-inch rectangles. Dip the knife in the hot water, make the first cut and wipe dry the knife. Repeat the dipping, cutting and drying process until you have cut the entire cake into bars. Cover the cake pan and return the cut bars to the freezer to freeze hard again, 2 to 3 hours.

CHOCOLATE "DIP" MIXTURE Fill a medium pot $\frac{1}{4}$ full with water, bring to a boil on high heat and then turn down the heat to a simmer. Combine the chocolate and cocoa butter in a small bowl, set it over the pot of simmering water and stir with a rubber spatula until the ingredients melt together. Once melted, prepare to dip the ice cream bars.

TO SERVE Have ready a wooden serving platter. Remove the ice cream bars from the freezer. Using your fingers, remove a bar from the cake pan and dip its top and sides in the warm chocolate mixture. Place the chocolate-dipped bar, undipped side down, on the platter and repeat until each bar has been coated. If the chocolate mixture starts to harden in the bowl, gently rewarm it before dipping the remaining bars.

Arrange the bars on a clean serving platter and garnish with the fresh cherries. Serve immediately.

warm chocolate tart with blackberries

PÂTE SUCRÉE Combine the butter and icing sugar in the bowl of a stand mixer fitted with the paddle attachment. Beat at medium speed until smooth, 2 to 3 minutes.

In a medium bowl, use a fork to gently mix together the egg yolks and water. With the mixer running at low speed, slowly add the egg mixture to the butter-sugar mixture until mostly incorporated, about 1 minute. Add ⅓ of the flour and continue mixing at low speed until smooth. Scrape down the sides of the bowl, add the remaining flour all at once and continue mixing until just incorporated. Do not overmix.

Remove the dough from the mixer and, using your hands, gently flatten and form it into a rough disk. Wrap the dough in plastic wrap and refrigerate for at least 1 hour before baking. This will keep in the fridge for 3 to 4 days, and can be frozen for up to 2 weeks.

Have ready a 10-inch tart tin with a removable bottom set on a baking tray. Lightly dust a clean work surface with flour, then unwrap the dough and discard the plastic wrap. Using a rolling pin lightly dusted with flour, roll the dough into a circle 14 inches in diameter and about ¼ inch thick. Keep the pastry as round and as even as possible. Wrap the pastry onto the rolling pin and transfer it to the tart tin, unrolling it and gently pressing the pastry into the pan. Allow any excess dough to hang over the edge of the pan. Refrigerate for 10 minutes.

pâte sucrée

¾ cup + 1 Tbsp unsalted butter, at room temperature

¾ cup icing sugar

3 egg yolks

3 Tbsp whole milk

2¾ cups all-purpose flour

We always like to give blackberries some love when they are in season, and we feel this warm chocolate tart is the perfect way to do so. As with most ingredients, using the best-quality chocolate you can afford will make a difference to the flavour of this tart. We like Valrhona, Lindt and other fine chocolates.

Preheat the oven to 350°F. To blind bake the pastry, line it with aluminum foil. Fill it with pie weights or baking beans and bake for 12 to 15 minutes, until the edges are golden brown. Gently remove the pie weights and foil and return the pastry to the oven for 5 to 6 minutes, or until it is lightly golden. Remove from the oven and set on a wire rack to cool.

CHOCOLATE FILLING Place the chocolate in a clean stainless steel bowl. Combine the milk and cream in a saucepan and bring to a boil on medium heat. Pour the hot cream mixture over the chocolate and whisk until melted. Add the eggs and whisk until well combined. Set aside until needed.

To assemble: Preheat the oven to 250°F. Set the cooled tart shell on a baking tray. Pour the chocolate filling into the tart, filling it all the way to the top of the pastry, and bake for 25 to 30 minutes, or until just set in the centre like a crème brûlée.

Remove from the oven and allow to cool for 15 to 20 minutes. While the tart is still slightly warm, remove the sides of the tart pan and cut into 8 to 12 wedges.

TO SERVE Place a wedge of tart on each individual plate. Garnish with blackberries, dust with icing sugar and top with a sprig of mint.

chocolate filling

18 oz Valrhona Equatoriale chocolate (or equivalent 55% cocoa dark chocolate), roughly chopped

¾ cup whole milk

1½ cups whipping cream

3 whole eggs, at room temperature

1½ cups fresh blackberries, for garnish

1 Tbsp icing sugar, for garnish

12 sprigs fresh mint, for garnish

orange marshmallow & chocolate treats

ORANGE MARSHMALLOW Spray a 9½ × 13-inch baking tray with nonstick spray and line it with parchment paper. Spray the parchment paper with a bit more of the nonstick spray. Set aside. Cut a second piece of parchment paper the same size as the first and set it aside too.

In a medium bowl, soak the gelatin sheets in enough cold water to cover until soft, about 5 minutes.

Place the granulated sugar in a small saucepan. Slowly add the water, adding just enough to moisten the sugar completely without leaving any dry spots. Add the honey and glucose (do not stir or the mixture may crystallize) and bring the mixture to a boil on high heat. Using a candy thermometer to check the temperature of the sugar mixture, once it reaches the soft-ball stage (240°F), remove it from the heat and allow it to cool to the boiling point, 212°F.

Using your hands, squeeze the excess water from the gelatin and transfer to the bowl of a stand mixer fitted with the whisk attachment. Carefully pour a small amount of syrup onto the gelatin and whisk at medium speed until the gelatin is fully dissolved, about 1 minute. Increase the speed of the mixer to medium-high and slowly and carefully add the rest of the syrup. Increase the speed to high and whip until the mixture is white and fluffy, 8 to 10 minutes. Add the orange zest and vanilla seeds with the Grand Marnier and mix at low speed to combine.

Using a rubber spatula, scrape the marshmallow onto the prepared baking tray, spreading it quickly and evenly. Spray one side of the reserved parchment paper with a small amount of nonstick spray and place it, spray side down, on top of the marshmallow. Let it stand at room temperature overnight to set.

orange marshmallow

11 sheets gelatin

1½ cups + 1 Tbsp granulated sugar

½ cup water

6 oz glucose

6 oz honey

Finely grated zest of 2 oranges

Seeds from ½ vanilla bean

2 tsp Grand Marnier

¼ cup cornstarch, for coating

¼ cup icing sugar, for coating

The recipe for the orange marshmallow is from Meagan Larmant, a pastry cook at Araxi. Here it is sandwiched between two biscuits and drizzled with chocolate sauce. For a crowd, make small canapé-sized versions topped with small pieces of candied orange zest or lightly sweetened whipped cream and serve with a glass of Grand Marnier.

Make the marshmallow the day before you plan to serve this dessert so it has time to set up overnight, then the rest of the dish comes together quickly. Glucose is available from many fine grocers, but if you can't find it, substitute light corn syrup instead.

SABLÉ BISCUIT DOUGH Combine the flour, icing sugar, salt and vanilla seeds in the bowl of a stand mixer fitted with the paddle attachment. Add the butter and mix at low speed until the mixture is crumbly in texture, 2 to 3 minutes. Add the egg yolks and mix at low speed until the mixture just comes together as a smooth mass, 2 to 3 minutes, scraping down the sides of the bowl as needed.

Place a large piece of plastic wrap on a clean work surface. Turn the dough out onto the plastic wrap and, using your hands, flatten it into a round disk. Wrap the dough completely in the plastic wrap and refrigerate for at least 1 hour. This will keep in the fridge for 3 to 4 days, and can be frozen for up to 2 weeks.

Line a nonstick baking tray with parchment paper. Remove the dough from the fridge and allow it to warm slightly at room temperature. Lightly dust a work surface with flour. Using a rolling pin lightly dusted with flour, roll the dough into a roughly 12 × 16-inch rectangle about ⅛ inch thick. Working quickly so the butter doesn't melt and and cause the dough to become tough, cut the dough into 24 rectangles. Transfer the biscuits to the lined baking tray and refrigerate for 15 minutes.

Preheat the oven to 325°F. Bake the sablé biscuits for 8 to 10 minutes, until light golden brown. Using an offset metal spatula, carefully transfer the biscuits to a wire cooling rack to cool completely before serving. *continued overleaf*

sablé biscuit dough

2 cups sifted all-purpose flour

¾ cup icing sugar, sifted

Small pinch of salt

Seeds from ½ vanilla bean

¾ cup + 1 Tbsp unsalted butter, at room temperature

2 egg yolks

semisweet chocolate sauce

8 oz dark chocolate (55 to 60% cocoa)

1 cup water

1 cup granulated sugar

2 tsp cocoa powder, sifted

¼ cup whipping cream

1 Tbsp Grand Marnier, or to taste

SEMISWEET CHOCOLATE SAUCE Combine the dark chocolate and water in a medium saucepan on low heat, stirring constantly with a heatproof rubber spatula until the chocolate is fully melted, about 5 minutes. Stir in the sugar and cocoa powder and bring to a boil on medium-high heat, again stirring constantly to ensure the sauce does not burn. Once the mixture comes to a boil, turn down the heat to medium-low and simmer for about 10 minutes until the mixture thickens slightly and becomes shiny.

Remove from the heat, pour in the cream and the Grand Marnier and mix to incorporate. Set aside in a warm place.

TO SERVE Using a sharp knife, cut the marshmallows into small rectangles, each ¾ of the height of the sablé biscuits but the same length. In a small bowl, combine the cornstarch and icing sugar and toss the marshmallows in this mixture. Shake off any excess. Use a small butane/propane torch to caramelize the surface of the marshmallows. Sandwich a marshmallow between 2 biscuits and drizzle with the chocolate sauce. Repeat with the remaining marshmallows, biscuits and chocolate sauce. Arrange on a serving platter.

longtable

ARAXI'S LONGTABLE DINNERS mark the height of the Sea-to-Sky summer. The first Longtable event, at Pemberton's strikingly beautiful North Arm Farm in 2011, was designed to show diners where Araxi's ingredients come from and to introduce them to local farmers, producers and winemakers. Now at least two dinners per year are held, each one in a different, but invariably breathtaking, outdoor location.

Whether on the shores of Whistler's Lost Lake or Vancouver's English Bay, one long table is adorned with white linen and fresh flowers and set with sparkling wine glasses and shining silverware for more than 200 guests. The night begins with a standing reception, where the guests are welcomed with a refreshing cocktail such as the Bramble On (made using the local artisan Schramm gin from Pemberton and blackberries fresh from the farm), along with opening tastes designed to wake the palate and introduce the flavour of both the season and the place.

Four courses, each served family-style and paired with BC wine, showcase the best of the region's produce, both the shoots and roots. The meal may begin with lightly fried squash blossoms stuffed with Dungeness crab, one of chef James Walt's signature dishes. To follow, perhaps a whole, salt-crusted wild salmon simply dressed with fresh herbs and an organic beef tenderloin served with ricotta gnudi. And to round out the meal, sweet and summery tartlets filled with raspberries picked from a nearby bush.

menu

COCKTAILS

Gin & Tonic   *Bramble On*

110-111

SMALL

112 Assorted Tomato
Salad & Crispy Squash
Blossoms

116 Ricotta Gnudi with
Peas & Mint

LARGER

120 Whole Wild Salmon
Baked in a Salt Crust

126 Whole Grilled Beef
Tenderloin with Green
Tomato Salsa

DESSERTS

Raspberry Tartlets

132

longtable

gin & tonic | MAKES 6

6 oz gin (we recommend
The Botanist or another varietal
with hints of citrus)

18 oz tonic water

Zest of 1 lemon (cut into long,
thin strips)

6 sprigs thyme

18 juniper berries

Have ready 6 highball glasses. Fill
a large pitcher with ice cubes and
add the gin. Insert a long bar spoon
and gently pour the tonic water
down the length of the spoon. This
will preserve the bubbles. Add the
lemon zest. Strain the mixture into
individual glasses and garnish with
a sprig of thyme and a few juniper
berries.

bramble on | MAKES 6

sage-infused simple syrup

5 oz Simple Syrup (page 219)

1 oz dried sage (or 6 sprigs fresh sage)

cocktail

30 fresh blackberries

2 cups ice cubes (plus more for serving)

6 oz gin

6 oz sloe gin

5 oz fresh lemon juice

5 oz sage-infused simple syrup

10 oz soda or sparkling water

6 sprigs sage, for garnish

SAGE-INFUSED SIMPLE SYRUP
Bring the simple syrup to a boil on high heat, add the sage and continue boiling for 1 minute. Remove from the heat and allow to cool. You can use the syrup as soon as it is cooled, but ideally, it should be steeped overnight (first remove and discard the fresh sprigs). This will keep refrigerated in an airtight container for up to 2 weeks.

COCKTAIL Have ready 6 Collins glasses. Add all but 6 of the blackberries to a pitcher and muddle. Add the ice and the gin, sloe gin, lemon juice and simple syrup, then stir until chilled and the blackberries are nicely agitated. Fill each glass ¾ full with ice, add ⅙ of the mixed alcohol and top with soda water (or sparkling water). Garnish with a fresh blackberry and a sprig of sage.

assorted tomato salad & crispy squash blossoms

CRISPY SQUASH BLOSSOMS Using a sharp knife, trim the blossom stems to ¼ inch and, if the fruit is attached, cut off and discard the end of the fruit and slice the squash once lengthwise to help it cook. Gently open the blossoms and cut out and discard the stamen. Gently brush out any dirt or insects inside the blossoms. Set them on a baking tray.

Combine the goat, White Grace (or cheddar) and Parmesan (or Grana Padano) cheeses and the riced potato in a large bowl and season lightly with salt and pepper. Let this stuffing stand in a warm place until soft, 10 to 15 minutes, then transfer it to a piping bag fitted with a wide nozzle. Insert the tip of the piping bag inside each blossom, filling each one ¾ full with the cheese mixture. Twist the top of each filled blossom to seal in the stuffing and place the filled blossoms back on the baking tray. Refrigerate until ready to serve.

ASSORTED TOMATO SALAD Slice and quarter the tomatoes according to their size and colour. Arrange them on a serving platter, season them evenly with salt and pepper and drizzle them with olive oil and balsamic crema (or vinegar). Tear the basil leaves and sprinkle them over the tomatoes along with the thyme leaves.

Finish the squash blossoms: Fill a deep pot or a wok two-thirds full with the oil and heat to 325°F (use a deep-fat thermometer to check the temperature).

crispy squash blossoms

12 summer squash or zucchini blossoms

4 oz soft goat cheese

2 oz White Grace or aged cheddar cheese, grated

2 oz Parmesan or Grana Padano cheese, grated

1 large yellow-fleshed potato (Kennebec or Yukon Gold), cooked and riced through a food mill

Sea salt and ground black pepper to taste

10 cups vegetable oil, for deep-frying

1 Tbsp chopped fresh chives

Pinch of freshly grated nutmeg

1 cup all-purpose flour

2 eggs, lightly beaten

¾ cup whole milk

1½ cups panko bread crumbs

We served this dish at our very first Longtable Dinner with Outstanding in the Field, a travelling group of chefs led by Jim Denevan who do pop-up longtable events throughout the US, Canada and Europe. Squash blossoms are very prolific: if you don't have any in your own garden, they are available at most farmers' markets. Or ask your friends—I'm sure someone has a few in their garden. They are a great vessel for a variety of fillings, including cheese, crab and other delicious things.

Place the flour in a bowl. Combine the eggs and milk in a second bowl and mix thoroughly. Place the bread crumbs in a third bowl. Dip the filled squash blossoms first into the flour and shake off the excess, then place them in the egg mixture and then, lastly, in the bread crumbs. Refrigerate half of the squash blossoms while you fry the rest.

Line a plate with paper towels. Quickly drop 6 of the blossoms into the hot oil, frying them until lightly golden and crispy, about 3 minutes. Using a slotted spoon, transfer the blossoms to the paper towels to drain. Remove the second batch of filled blossoms from the fridge, drop them into the hot oil and fry until golden and crispy, about 3 minutes. Transfer them to the paper towels. Lightly season the blossoms with salt.

TO SERVE Arrange the crispy squash blossoms on top of the tomato salad and serve immediately.

assorted tomato salad

3 to 4 lb assorted fresh tomatoes

Sea salt and cracked black pepper to taste

¼ cup good-quality extra-virgin olive oil

2 Tbsp balsamic crema or syrupy aged balsamic vinegar

10 fresh basil leaves

1 tsp fresh thyme leaves

These tender, gnocchi-like pasta dumplings are perfect little flavour catchers. In this recipe, fresh peas and mint highlight the tangy ricotta cheese. You can find buffalo ricotta cheese in local cheese shops or Italian grocers, but cow's milk ricotta can work just as well. If you are in a hurry, use your favourite pasta noodle instead of the gnudi and use good-quality frozen peas if fresh are not available.

SERVES 8 TO 10 AS A SIDE DISH (MAKES 60 TO 72 PIECES)

ricotta gnudi with peas & mint

In a large bowl, mix together the whole milk (or buffalo) ricotta, eggs, olive oil and salt until thoroughly combined. Add 2 cups of the "00" flour all at once and, using a pastry cutter or a fork, gently and swiftly work it into a soft dough. Using your hands, gently gather the dough into a ball, wrap it in plastic wrap and refrigerate for at least 30 minutes.

Lightly dust a clean work surface and a large plate or baking tray with flour. Divide the dough into 4 roughly equal parts. Roll each piece between your palms to form a log about 1 inch in diameter. Place the logs on the counter and, using a pastry scraper or paring knife, cut each one into 1-inch pieces. (You will have about 15 to 18 per log, or 60 to 72 pieces total.) Arrange the gnudi in a single layer on the baking tray and refrigerate for at least 30 minutes or until needed. You can freeze the gnudi at this point for up to 1 month.

Bring a large pot of salted water to a boil on high heat. Bring the vegetable nage to a simmer in a large sauté pan on medium-high heat, cook for 3 to 4 minutes until reduced by ½, then add the butter. When the butter has melted, add the peas.

Add ½ of the gnudi to the boiling salted water and cook until they float to the surface, 2 to 3 minutes. Using a slotted spoon, add them to the peas. Cook the second batch of gnudi and add them to the peas too. Once all the gnudi have been cooked and added to the pan, remove from the heat and stir in the mint. Season lightly with sea salt, then transfer to a serving bowl. Serve topped with the ricotta salata.

2 lb whole milk or buffalo ricotta, drained

2 large eggs, lightly beaten

2 Tbsp extra-virgin olive oil

2 tsp kosher or sea salt

2 cups + 3 Tbsp Italian "00" flour (see page 77)

¾ cup Vegetable Nage (page 220)

2 Tbsp unsalted butter

1½ cups fresh or thawed frozen peas, blanched

2 Tbsp chopped fresh mint

½ cup grated ricotta salata

whole wild salmon baked in a salt crust

Baking any fish, not just salmon, in a salt crust is a great way to keep it nice and moist, especially because it's left on the bone. And cracking into the salt crust provides just the kind of dramatic presentation that everybody loves. Don't be afraid of the salt part, because the fish does not taste salty at all.

Preheat the oven to 400°F. Place the egg whites in a large bowl and whisk for 1 minute. Add all of the coarse salt along with ¼ cup of cold water and mix thoroughly.

Arrange about ½ of the salt mixture down the centre of a baking tray that is slightly larger than the salmon. Create a trench large enough to hold the salmon, and set the fish on top. Open the belly cavity, arrange the dill and lemon slices inside and drizzle with the olive oil. Season lightly with the fine salt. Close the belly cavity and mound the remaining salt mixture over the salmon as evenly as possible. Use your hands to shape and lightly press the salt together, ensuring that it completely covers the fish. Bake for 25 minutes. To check for doneness, insert a skewer or the tip of a knife through the crust and into the thickest part of the fish near the head. If the skewer (or knife) is warm when you pull it out, it is done. If not, return the fish to the oven for 5 more minutes. Remove the salmon from the oven and let it stand for 10 to 15 minutes.

TO SERVE I like to bring the tray to the table, crack the salt crust and then remove the crust to fully expose the fish. Before serving, I remove the dill and lemons from the belly cavity and discard them. I peel away and discard the fish skin and, using a knife or a spoon, loosen the fillet from along the spine. Using a spatula or a large spoon, I remove the top fillet and transfer it to a serving platter. Then I remove the spine and rib cage to expose the bottom fillet, removing it down to the skin and placing it alongside the top fillet on the platter. Pass around the platter with a bowl of dill dressing so guests can help themselves.

4 egg whites
4 lb coarse sea salt
1 wild salmon (sockeye, coho or chinook), 6 to 7 lb, scales and gills removed
4 sprigs dill
1 lemon, sliced
1 Tbsp extra-virgin olive oil
1 recipe Dill Dressing (page 145)
Pinch of fine sea salt

This is a great outdoor dish. Although tenderloin is always a splurge, the lean meat pairs really well with the green tomato salsa. And the salsa is the perfect way to use up any tomatoes in your garden that no longer seem to ripen once the weather cools. Serve this recipe with the ricotta gnudi or your favourite potato or pasta dish. I even like it with a simple green salad, since meat does not always need potatoes.

SERVES 8

whole grilled beef tenderloin with green tomato salsa

GREEN TOMATO SALSA Preheat the barbecue or an indoor grill to medium-high heat. In a medium bowl, toss the tomatoes (or tomatillos), shallots, garlic and jalapeño with 3 Tbsp of the olive oil. Place these vegetables on the grill and cook for 4 to 5 minutes. Using tongs, transfer the cooked vegetables to a plate and allow them to cool.

Once cooled, place the grilled vegetables in a blender or food processor along with the remaining olive oil and the cilantro, parsley and vinegar. Blend at high speed until smooth, about 3 minutes, season with salt and pepper and mix to incorporate. Pour the salsa into a serving bowl and refrigerate until needed. This will keep refrigerated in an airtight container for about 2 days, after which it will start to lose its green freshness.

GRILLED BEEF TENDERLOIN Preheat your barbecue or indoor grill to medium-high heat. Have ready some butcher's twine and an instant-read meat thermometer.

Set the tenderloin on a clean work surface. Cut about 7 pieces of butcher's twine, each about 8 inches long. Starting at one end, tie a piece of butcher's twine around the beef 2 inches from the end. Measure another 2 inches in from the first piece of twine and tie a second piece around the beef. Repeat every 2 inches until the beef is tightly rolled and tied. This step promotes even cooking by maintaining a similar thickness of meat throughout. (If the end is quite thin, fold it underneath to create a double layer of meat and tie it in place.) Drizzle the tied meat with the olive oil and season it with the pepper and a generous amount of sea salt. *continued overleaf*

green tomato salsa

12 medium green tomatoes or tomatillos, cut in half

4 medium shallots, peeled and cut in half

3 cloves garlic, cut in half

1 green jalapeño pepper, cut in half and seeds removed

1 cup extra-virgin olive oil, divided

1 cup cilantro, leaves and stems

1 cup flat-leaf parsley, stems removed

2 Tbsp red wine vinegar

Sea salt and ground black pepper to taste

grilled beef tenderloin

1 whole grass-fed beef tenderloin, 4 to 5 lb, peeled of sinew and silverskin

2 Tbsp extra-virgin olive oil

1 Tbsp cracked black pepper

Sea salt to taste

Sear the tenderloin on the grill for about 4 minutes, then turn the meat over and cook for a further 4 minutes. Repeat to sear the 2 remaining sides. (You will sear the beef for a total of about 16 minutes at this stage.) Turn down the heat to low and cook the meat for a further 10 to 15 minutes, turning it every 2 to 3 minutes. To test for doneness, insert the thermometer into the thickest part of the tenderloin. Once it registers 125 to 130°F for medium rare, transfer the meat to a cooling rack and let rest in a warm place for about 15 minutes.

TO SERVE Using a sharp knife, slice the beef into ⅛-inch slices. Arrange the meat slices on a warm platter and serve with the green tomato salsa.

JORDAN AND TRISH STURDY of North Arm Farm have been helping Araxi connect to the soil since chef James Walt first arrived in 1997. Because the 55-acre farm was so large and the output so dependable, it was the first place that made James feel absolutely confident about local sourcing in the Sea-to-Sky region. Today the farm supplies the restaurant like a pantry with produce ranging from beans, salsify, cabbage and cauliflower to garlic, kale, parsnips and squash. Of particular note are the summer raspberries and strawberries, which brighten muddled cocktails, anchor or complement desserts, and sweeten mignonettes that dress freshly shucked oysters. The farm's tomatoes also anchor salads, gazpachos and sauces; amplify marmalades and green salsas; and complement squash blossoms and golden brown arancini. With stunning Mt. Currie as a backdrop, the farm's view is one of the most picturesque in British Columbia and made it the natural choice for Araxi's first-ever Longtable Dinner in 2011. And in addition to farming, Jordan, formerly a 3-term mayor of Pemberton, now represents the whole Sea-to-Sky region in the provincial legislature.

araxi | **GOING TO THE SOURCE**

raspberry
tartlets

PÂTE SUCRÉE Combine the butter and icing sugar in the bowl of a stand mixer fitted with the paddle attachment. Beat at medium speed until smooth, 2 to 3 minutes.

In a medium bowl, whisk together the egg yolks and water. With the mixer running at low speed, slowly add the egg mixture to the butter-sugar mixture until mostly incorporated, about 1 minute. Add ⅓ of the flour and mix at low speed until smooth, about 1 minute. Add the remaining flour all at once and continue mixing until fully incorporated. Do not overmix.

Remove the dough from the mixer and, using your hands, divide it into 6 pieces. Gently flatten each piece slightly, wrap it in plastic wrap and refrigerate for at least 1 hour before rolling.

ORANGE-SCENTED PASTRY CREAM Combine the milk, half of the sugar and the vanilla bean in a medium saucepan and bring to a boil on medium heat. Using a slotted spoon, remove and discard the vanilla pod.

In a large bowl, whisk together the egg yolks and the remaining sugar until smooth and creamy. Add the flour and cornstarch and whisk again until smooth. Gradually pour the scalded milk into the yolk mixture, whisking constantly until smooth. Return the custard mixture to the pot and bring to a boil on medium-high heat, whisking constantly and vigorously to prevent the pastry cream from burning. Once the mixture reaches a boil, turn down the heat to medium-low and simmer for 1 minute. Remove from the heat.

Stir the orange zest, 1 Tbsp of the Grand Marnier and the butter into the pastry cream, then whisk until smooth. Transfer the mixture to a bowl and cover with plastic wrap, pressing the plastic wrap right against the surface of the cream so it does not form a skin. Refrigerate until cold, about 1 hour.

pâte sucrée

¾ cup + 1 Tbsp unsalted butter, at room temperature

¾ cup icing sugar

3 egg yolks

3 Tbsp whole milk

2¾ cups all-purpose flour

orange-scented pastry cream

2 cups whole milk

½ cup granulated sugar

1 vanilla bean, split lengthwise and seeds scraped

6 egg yolks

¼ cup sifted all-purpose flour

1 Tbsp cornstarch

Zest of 1 orange

2 Tbsp Grand Marnier

1 Tbsp unsalted butter, softened

3 pints fresh raspberries, for garnish

1 Tbsp Simple Syrup (page 219), for garnish

Always an Araxi Longtable Dinner favourite, these mini pies are filled with an orange-scented pastry cream that really highlights the lovely tartness of the raspberries. Feel free to substitute your own family pastry recipe for the pâte sucrée, if you prefer.

FINISH TARTLETS Have ready six 4-inch tart tins set on a baking tray. Lightly dust a clean work surface with flour, then unwrap the dough and discard the plastic wrap. Using a rolling pin, roll each piece into a circle 6 inches in diameter and about ⅛ inch thick. Keep the pastry as round and as even as possible. Wrap each piece of pastry onto the rolling pin and then transfer it to a tart tin, unrolling it and gently pressing the pastry into the pan. Allow any excess dough to hang over the edge of the mould. Refrigerate for 10 minutes.

Preheat the oven to 350°F. To blind bake the pastry, line it with aluminum foil. Fill it with pie weights or baking beans and bake for 15 minutes, until the edges are golden brown. Gently remove the pie weights and foil and return the pastry to the oven for 4 to 6 minutes, or until it is lightly golden. Remove from the oven and set the pastry on a wire rack to cool to room temperature.

Remove the pastry cream from the fridge and whisk it until smooth. Using a spatula, divide it evenly among the tart shells, filling them to just below the rim. Refrigerate for 15 minutes or until ready to serve.

TO SERVE In a small bowl, gently toss the fresh raspberries with the simple syrup and the remaining 1 Tbsp of the Grand Marnier until well coated. Arrange the raspberries in pyramid-like mounds on top of each filled tart. Serve at room temperature.

roots

WHISTLER IS AN alpine paradise from November to April, when its annual average snowfall of almost 38 feet draws millions of skiers and snowboarders from around the world and it plays host to World Cup events, Pride parties and snowsports celebrations. Outside of ski season, the village attracts visitors from far and wide to film festivals, bicycle races, half-marathons, and hugely popular food and wine events.

Expectations are high, and with Araxi's reputation for excellence, visitors expect the best of local food even when the surrounding farmland lies under a thick blanket of snow. Sourcing local food during the colder months in British Columbia is a tall order, but the cooks are more than prepared, using foods—crosnes, salsify, carrots, beets, leeks, mushrooms, sunchokes and much more—that they have foraged, cellared, pickled and preserved during the warmer months.

In addition, they seek out pine, chanterelle and lobster mushrooms; embrace winter vegetables, including the valley's famous potatoes; slow-cook local, grass-fed beef; pan-roast and confit duck from Yarrow Meadows; and dip into British Columbia's cold waters for oysters, steelhead, sablefish and sturgeon. Winter, for the kitchen brigade at Araxi, is a season of challenge and creativity that the chefs meet head on.

menu

COCKTAILS

Harmonious Shake   *Sin City*

Up The Creek   *Firecracker Margarita*

140-143

SMALL

144 Baby Gem Lettuce with Dill Dressing

146 I Love Brussels Sprouts

147 Carrot & Coriander Soup

149 Roasted Beets with Chickpea Caponata & Nasturtium Pesto

153 Wild Mushroom Velouté

154 Sautéed Wild Mushrooms with Soft-Boiled Eggs

156 Grilled Bread with Romesco & Manchego Cheese

157 Albacore Tuna in Olive Oil, Lemon & Herbs

158 Chilled Oysters with Three Mignonettes

160 Geoduck Clams with Shaved Fennel & Apple Dressing

162 Grilled Octopus "Jorge Style"

166 Crispy Oyster "Po' Boy" Tacos & Salsa Verde

168 Dungeness Crab Cakes with Corn Salsa

LARGER

171 Seared Wild Scallops with Cauliflower Tempura

174 Oysters Baked in Seaweed with Fonduto

177 Scallops in the Shell with Sea Urchin Butter

178 Roasted Sablefish Tail on Root Vegetables

180 Sunshine Coast Sturgeon & Caviar with Beet Salsa

184 Araxi Après Fondue

186 Seared Duck Breasts with Fresh Horseradish & Sesame

189 Mark's Rabbit Sausage

192 "Stretch the Steak" Tartine with Aged Provolone

194 Fresh Bacon with Carrots & Mustard Vinaigrette

197 Slow-Cooked Beef Cheeks in Port Wine

200 Braised Lamb Shanks with Carrot Purée

DESSERTS

202 Vanilla Doughnuts with Earl Grey Tea Ice Cream

206 Maple Sugar Crème Brûlées with Shortbread

208 Apple & Almond Tart with Whipped Sour Cream

212 Sour Cream Coffee Cake with Poached Pears

214 Dark Chocolate Mousse Coupes

roots

For a lighter version of this shake, feel free to add two cups of club soda, which will carbonate and slightly dilute it.

harmonious shake | MAKES 6

1 English cucumber, skin on

2 cups ice cubes

12 oz steeped camomile tea, chilled

6 oz Hendrick's gin

6 oz cold sake

4 oz fresh lemon juice

4 oz elderflower cordial

Have ready 6 Collins glasses. Slice the cucumber in half widthwise. Chop one half into 6 to 8 pieces. In a pitcher, muddle the cucumber pieces. Add the ice and all of the liquid ingredients and stir until well chilled. Fill each glass ¾ full of ice and strain the mixture over it. Slice the remaining half-cucumber lengthwise into 6 long, flat strips. Garnish each glass by placing a slice of cucumber between the ice and the side of the glass.

sin city | MAKES 6

10 oz brewed espresso coffee, chilled

5 oz vanilla vodka

5 oz Kahlúa

5 oz Bailey's Irish Cream

6 cups ice cubes

Chocolate syrup, for the rim

Shaved or grated bittersweet chocolate, for the rim (optional)

Chill 6 martini glasses in the freezer. In a pitcher, combine ⅓ of all the liquid ingredients with 2 cups of the ice and shake well. Rim 2 glasses with chocolate syrup (and dip in shaved chocolate if desired), then pour the mixture into individual glasses. Repeat twice more with the remaining ingredients.

Adjust the level of Chartreuse in this recipe according to your preference. If you enjoy it, spray or soak the apple slices in Chartreuse for extra flavour.

up the creek | MAKES 6

cedar plank–infused rye

1 bottle (750 mL) rye

3 small pieces clean cedar plank

cocktail

12 oz cedar plank-infused rye

6 oz apple juice

3 oz fresh lime juice

3 oz maple syrup

1 to 1½ oz green Chartreuse

3 cups ice cubes

1 apple, skin on, cut into thin slices (I like to use pink lady or ambrosia)

CEDAR PLANK–INFUSED RYE
In a sterilized 4-cup airtight container, pour the rye over the cedar pieces and let them infuse for at least 72 hours, or even better, 1 week. Remove and discard the cedar. Pour the rye into a sterilized airtight bottle. This will keep in the bottle for up to 3 months.

COCKTAIL Have ready 6 highball glasses. In a pitcher, combine all of the liquid ingredients with the ice and stir until well chilled. Pour into glasses, topping with more ice if needed. Garnish each glass with a slice of apple.

An accompanying shot of milk makes a nice complement to the spicy heat of this drink.

firecracker margarita

MAKES 6

infused tequila

1 bottle (750 mL) silver tequila

1 oz hibiscus flower water

5 jalapeño peppers, with seeds, each sliced lengthwise into 3 or 4 pieces

10 basil leaves

firecracker margarita

Smoked sea salt, for the rim

6 jalapeño peppers

20 medium basil leaves

1 orange, cut into 6 wedges

3 cups ice cubes

10 oz infused tequila

8 oz fresh lime juice

4 oz Cointreau

4 oz Simple Syrup (page 219)

6 shots milk, each 1 oz (optional)

INFUSED TEQUILA In a 4-cup sterilized airtight bottle, mix all of the ingredients together and let them infuse for 48 hours. This will keep in the bottle for up to 3 months.

FIRECRACKER MARGARITA Have ready 6 highball glasses rimmed with the smoked sea salt.

Slice the top quarter off the jalapeños and slit each top for a garnish. Slice each jalapeño lengthwise into 3 to 4 pieces and place in a pitcher with its seeds. Slap the basil between your palms to release the oils and add to the pitcher. Squeeze the juice from the 6 orange wedges into the pitcher. Add the ice, infused tequila, lime juice, Cointreau and simple syrup and stir well.

Pour the mixture into the salt-rimmed glasses, leaving in the jalapeños and basil for a rustic feel. Garnish each glass with a sliced jalapeño top.

This simple salad combines a few of my favourite things: a comforting ranch-like dill dressing, hard Italian cheese and gem lettuce. A cross between romaine and iceberg varieties, gem lettuce can be served raw or cooked or grilled.

baby gem lettuce with dill dressing

DILL DRESSING   Combine all of the ingredients in a small bowl and whisk together until well combined. Adjust the seasoning as needed. This will keep refrigerated in an airtight container for up to 1 week.

GEM LETTUCE SALAD   Place a serving platter in the fridge to chill. To prepare the lettuce, peel away any rough or wilted outer leaves, cut the lettuce heads in quarters and wash them in cold water. Arrange the heads upside down in a bowl or on a baking tray and refrigerate them until well drained, about 10 minutes. Cut the tomatoes in wedges and cut the eggs in half then into wedges.

To assemble the salad, randomly place the lettuce wedges on the chilled platter. Lightly drizzle a little dill dressing on top. Drape the prosciutto (or ham) over the lettuce and scatter the egg wedges and tomato wedges over the salad. Drizzle with more dill dressing. Using a microplane or a grater, top the salad with some Parmigiano-Reggiano (or Grana Padano) cheese, then drizzle with olive oil. Serve chilled.

dill dressing

1 cup buttermilk

½ cup mayonnaise

Juice of 1 lemon

¼ cup skim milk powder

¼ cup chopped flat-leaf parsley

2 Tbsp chopped dill

1 Tbsp Dijon mustard

1½ tsp onion powder

Sea salt and ground black pepper to taste

gem lettuce salad

4 to 5 heads of baby gem lettuce

7 to 8 slices very good prosciutto, serrano, speck or smoked ham

4 eggs, cooked in boiling water for 8 minutes, cooled and peeled

2 ripe tomatoes

2 oz Parmigiano-Reggiano or Grana Padano cheese

2 Tbsp good-quality extra-virgin olive oil

I love brussels sprouts

The name of this dish says it all. Ever since I was a little kid, I have loved Brussels sprouts. Although this recipe makes a great side dish for the Whole Grilled Beef Tenderloin (page 126) or Whole Wild Salmon Baked in a Salt Crust (page 120), I like to eat it with just a crisp salad and some good bread. Make sure you take the time to roast the Brussels sprouts to draw their flavour out. Use good prosciutto as well.

Fill a medium saucepan with lightly salted water and bring to a boil on high heat. Add the Brussels sprouts and cook for 6 to 7 minutes, until tender. Drain them and set aside.

Preheat the oven to 375°F. In an ovenproof skillet on medium heat, melt the butter with the olive oil. Stir in the Brussels sprouts to coat them and sauté for 5 to 6 minutes, until they begin to brown. Season with the salt and pepper, then deglaze the pan with the balsamic vinegar, cooking it for 2 to 3 minutes until it evaporates. Remove the skillet from the heat.

Drape the prosciutto over the sprouts and place the skillet in the oven for 8 to 10 minutes, until the meat starts to shrink and turn light brown around the edges. Remove from the oven, scoop into a serving bowl and serve immediately (making sure that everyone gets some crispy prosciutto).

2½ lb Brussels sprouts, outer leaves discarded, cut in half
¼ cup unsalted butter
1 Tbsp extra-virgin olive oil
½ tsp sea salt
½ tsp ground black pepper
3 Tbsp balsamic vinegar
6 thin slices prosciutto

This is a very simple soup and one that my kids have always loved. It's also a great way to use up carrots, which can take over a farm garden pretty quickly. You can make this soup in larger batches and freeze some for rainy days.

carrot & coriander soup

In a large saucepan, melt the butter with the olive oil on medium heat. Add the onions and cook for 8 to 10 minutes, until soft and translucent, then stir in the garlic and coriander seeds and cook for 3 to 4 minutes to toast the coriander. Add the carrots then the stock and bring to a boil. Turn down the heat to low, cover the pot and cook until the carrots are tender, about 15 minutes. Remove from the heat and stir in the milk, honey and nutmeg.

Working in batches if necessary, carefully pour the soup into a blender or food processor and purée at high speed until smooth. Season with salt and white pepper. Place a fine-mesh sieve over another pot and strain the soup. Discard any solids. Reheat if necessary. And remember, hot soup should be served in hot bowls. Garnish with the chopped cilantro.

¼ cup butter

1 Tbsp extra-virgin olive oil

2 medium white onions, sliced

2 cloves garlic, sliced

1 tsp coriander seeds

4 lb local carrots, peeled and roughly chopped

8 cups vegetable stock

1½ cups whole milk

¾ cup honey

2 pinches fresh nutmeg

Sea salt and cracked white pepper to taste

2 Tbsp chopped cilantro

CARROT &
CORIANDER SOUP
page 147

ROASTED BEETS WITH
CHICKPEA CAPONATA
& NASTURTIUM PESTO
page 150

149

roasted beets with chickpea caponata & nasturtium pesto

ROASTED BEETS Preheat the oven to 375°F. Cut 2 pieces of aluminum foil, each 10 × 12 inches, and place one on top of the other. Place the beets in the centre of the foil and add the oil, thyme, garlic and salt. Fold the foil around the beets and roll up the edges to create a sealed package. Set the beets on a baking tray and roast for 30 to 40 minutes. To check for doneness, remove the beets from the oven, carefully unwrap them and insert the tip of a knife into one of them. The knife should slide easily in and out.

When the beets are cooked, remove them from the oven, unwrap and discard the foil and set aside the beets until they are just cool enough to handle. Using your fingers or a dishtowel, rub the beets to loosen their skins. Peel and discard the skins. Set aside to cool.

NASTURSIUM PESTO Have ready a large bowl of ice water. Bring a large saucepan of salted water to a boil on high heat. Add the nasturtium leaves and cook for 20 seconds. Using a slotted spoon, transfer the nasturtium leaves to the ice water to stop the cooking. When the leaves are cool, drain them and pat them with paper towels to remove any excess moisture.

Place the nasturtium leaves, grapeseed (or canola) oil and garlic in a blender or food processor and blend at high speed for 1 minute until smooth. With the motor turned off, add the cheese, nuts and lemon zest then process at high speed for a further 30 seconds until thickened. Pour into a bowl and refrigerate until needed. This will keep refrigerated in an airtight container for 2 or 3 days.

roasted beets

1 lb assorted beets (golden, red or Chioggia), washed and dried with paper towels

3 Tbsp grapeseed or canola oil

3 sprigs thyme

2 cloves garlic, unpeeled

Pinch of coarse sea salt

nasturtium pesto

1 cup firmly packed nasturtium leaves, washed, + 10 to 12 smaller leaves, for garnish

1/3 cup grapeseed or canola oil

2 cloves garlic, crushed with the side of a knife

¼ cup grated Pecorino-Romano cheese

3 Tbsp toasted pecans or walnut pieces

Zest of ½ lemon

Our non-traditional take on a caponata uses chickpeas instead of eggplant but retains all the sweet and sour flavour. Nasturtiums are fantastic, and I always love the look on people's faces when they first eat one of these flowers. Where do you find them? Look no farther than your neighbour's garden or the farmers' market. While you're there, pick up some beets: we like ours somewhere between the size of a golf ball and a pool ball so they roast evenly.

CHICKPEA CAPONATA Heat the olive oil in a medium saucepan on medium heat. Add the red onion, garlic, bay leaves, coriander and chili flakes and cook for 4 to 5 minutes, until the onion has softened and the garlic is fragrant. Stir in the chickpeas, tomatoes and raisins and cook for 3 minutes to let the flavours combine. Remove from the heat and refrigerate until cool. Stir in the olives and parsley.

TO SERVE Place 1 Tbsp of the nasturtium pesto in the centre of each plate. Spread it across the plate with the back of the spoon. Top with 3 or 4 Tbsp of the chickpea caponata. Cut the beets into slices or quarters and arrange them on top of the chickpeas. Drizzle with the remaining pesto and garnish with nasturtium leaves. Serve immediately.

chickpea caponata

3 Tbsp good-quality extra-virgin olive oil

½ medium red onion, finely chopped

2 cloves garlic, finely chopped

2 bay leaves

1 tsp crushed coriander seeds

Pinch of red chili flakes

3 cups cooked chickpeas

½ cup fresh cherry tomatoes, cut in half

½ cup sultana raisins, soaked in hot water then drained

½ cup kalamata olives, pitted and roughly chopped

1 Tbsp chopped curly-leaf parsley

araxi | **GOING TO THE SOURCE**

KNOWN TO LOCALS as Spud Valley, the Pemberton Valley north of Whistler is officially the Seed Potato Capital of North America, and has been since 1945. Careful monitoring keeps the region's 27 potato varieties pure and the area isolated from viruses. Araxi serves more than 20,000 pounds of potatoes per year and buys a fair portion of them from potato farmers Bruce and Brenda Miller and their five sons at Across the Creek Organics in Pemberton Meadows. Of the nearly dozen varieties they grow on 500 acres between the Lillooet River and Ryan Creek, the German Butters are a favourite to serve on their own or in gnocchi, and the Kennebecs make great fries.

MANY OF THE cooks at Araxi are mushroom foragers. From October through November, the forests all along the Sea-to-Sky Corridor are full of white chanterelle, pine and lobster mushrooms, while April is all about morels. Restaurant staff can often be spotted wandering the woods on their days off with a basket and fungi knives in hand; most of their harvest, however, ends up in staff meals, and Araxi relies on James Town, a former Toptable Group sous chef, and the foragers at Mikuni Wild Harvest to keep the restaurant supplied. Nearly 90% of mushrooms eaten in North America every year are cultivated white button mushrooms; but once you taste the earthy flavours of locally foraged varieties, there's no going back!

In the fall, you'll find people foraging for wild mushrooms all along the Sea-to-Sky Corridor, and a lot of our young chefs spend their time off in the woods around Whistler and Pemberton doing just that. The great thing about wild mushrooms is that each type brings a different flavour. This recipe is best with a mix of chanterelles, morels and cauliflower or coral mushrooms. I find pine mushrooms are best on their own. Serve this soup with crusty, toasted or garlic bread.

SERVES
6 TO 8

wild mushroom velouté

In a large saucepan, melt the butter with the olive oil on medium heat. Add the shallots and cook for 5 minutes, until softened and lightly coloured. Stir in the garlic then the mushrooms, season with salt and cook for 6 to 8 minutes, until the mushrooms are golden brown and the garlic is fragrant.

Add the bay leaves and thyme and increase the heat to high. Pour in the vermouth and sherry and cook, stirring occasionally, until all of the liquid has evaporated, 7 to 8 minutes. Add the hot stock, bring to a boil, turn down the heat to medium-low and simmer, uncovered, for 8 to 10 minutes to concentrate the flavours.

Stir in the cream and let the soup simmer for 1 minute. Remove from the heat, then spoon out and discard the bay leaves.

Working in batches if necessary, carefully pour the soup into a blender and purée at high speed until smooth. Season with salt and pepper. Place a medium-fine sieve over a clean bowl and strain the soup. Discard the solids. Ladle into deep bowls and serve nice and hot.

¼ cup butter

1 Tbsp extra-virgin olive oil

6 large shallots, thinly sliced

2 cloves garlic, sliced

5 cups assorted wild mushrooms, cleaned of dirt with a moist towel or brush and roughly chopped

Sea salt and ground black pepper to taste

3 bay leaves

2 sprigs thyme, leaves only

2 cups vermouth

1 cup dry sherry

8 cups hot vegetable or chicken stock

3 cups whipping cream

sautéed wild mushrooms with soft-boiled eggs

I love this dish for its simplicity. Fresh eggs and foraged mushrooms make a great fall meal that comes together quickly. Make sure to get a nice golden brown on the mushrooms, as this caramelization really highlights the earthy flavours.

SAUTÉED WILD MUSHROOMS Using a brush or a moist towel, remove any dirt or sand from the mushrooms. Using a sharp knife, quarter and slice the mushrooms. Create a rustic blend of sizes and shapes. Set aside.

Place a large sauté pan on medium-high heat and, once heated, add 2 Tbsp of the olive oil. Add all of the mushrooms, season them with salt to draw out the moisture, and cook until they have softened and the natural juices have almost cooked off, 4 to 5 minutes. Turn down the heat to medium and add the shallots and garlic, mixing them thoroughly into the mushrooms. Cook until the mushrooms are golden brown and you can clearly smell the garlic and shallots. Remove the pan from the heat and set aside in a warm place. Once the mushrooms have slightly cooled, add the parsley and mix thoroughly.

SOFT-BOILED EGGS Have ready a large bowl of cold water. Fill a medium saucepan with water and bring it to a boil on high heat. Using a slotted spoon, gently lower the eggs into the boiling water. Turn down the heat to medium and cook the eggs in the simmering water for 7 minutes and 45 seconds. Using the slotted spoon, transfer the eggs to the cold water until they are cool enough to handle, about 2 minutes.

TO SERVE Arrange the sautéed mushrooms on individual plates or on a serving platter and scatter the kale leaves over top. Gently crack and peel the eggs, discarding the shells and rinsing the eggs in water. Randomly place the eggs on the plates or platter and, using a sharp paring knife, cut into each egg just enough to reveal the soft yolk. Drizzle evenly with the remaining 2 Tbsp olive oil and sprinkle with chopped chives, black pepper and a little sea salt. Enjoy!

sautéed wild mushrooms

3 cups assorted wild mushrooms (chanterelles, porcini, black trumpet or morels)

4 Tbsp extra-virgin olive oil

Sea salt to taste

2 medium shallots, minced

2 cloves garlic, minced

2 Tbsp chopped curly-leaf parsley

1 cup baby kale leaves

soft-boiled eggs

6 hen eggs

1 Tbsp chopped fresh chives

Sea salt and crushed black pepper to taste

This dish is a *montadito*, a small toast topped with delicious ingredients and served tapas-style in Spain, and was inspired by our neighbouring sister restaurant, Bar Oso. And really, who doesn't like saying the word "montadito"? We keep this version quite classic with romesco sauce and Spanish Manchego cheese, but you could use nasturtium or basil pesto and fresh local goat cheese instead.

SERVES
8 TO 10
AS A
CANAPÉ

grilled bread with romesco & manchego cheese

Preheat the barbecue or an indoor grill on medium heat. Slice the baguettes into ¼-inch slices on the bias and place them on a baking tray. Using a pastry brush, baste the bread slices as evenly as possible with 2 Tbsp of the olive oil, then season the bread with salt and pepper.

Place ½ of the bread on the barbecue and cook on one side for 2 to 3 minutes, until golden and lightly charred. Turn the bread over and cook for another 2 to 3 minutes. Transfer the grilled bread to a plate and set aside in a warm place. Grill the remaining bread.

TO SERVE Arrange the slices of grilled bread in a single layer on a bread board or serving platter. Place a spoonful of romesco sauce on each slice of bread, then top evenly with the Manchego cheese. Drizzle with the remaining olive oil and serve.

2 baguettes (can be a day old)

4 Tbsp good-quality extra-virgin olive oil

Sea salt and cracked black pepper to taste

1 recipe Romesco Sauce (page 221)

7 oz Manchego cheese, shaved with a vegetable peeler or a sharp knife

This recipe is a bit different from the others in this book because it's a short-term preserving recipe. Once you have it in your fridge, you'll find yourself making it part of a Niçoise salad, mixing it with mayonnaise to spread over crusty bread, or, my personal favourite, adding it to warm boiled potatoes with lots of chopped parsley and lemon.

albacore tuna in olive oil, lemon & herbs

In a high-sided saucepan, combine the olive oil, lemon slices, garlic, shallots, salt, thyme, bay leaves and coriander on medium-low heat. Use a deep-fat thermometer to check the temperature of the oil. Once the oil reaches 140 to 150°F, cook for about 30 minutes.

Add the tuna after 30 minutes and keep checking the temperature until the oil returns to 140 to 150°F. Once the oil reaches this temperature, remove the pot from the heat, cover and let stand in a cool place for 10 minutes.

Have ready four sterilized 5 oz jars with tight-fitting lids. Using a slotted spoon, transfer the tuna to the jars. Place a fine-mesh sieve over a jar and strain the oil over the cooked tuna to cover it. Repeat with the other 3 jars. Discard the solids. Refrigerate the tuna until cool, then cover with a lid and seal tightly. This will keep refrigerated for 7 to 10 days.

TO SERVE Serve the tuna warm on its own or mixed into other dishes.

3 cups good-quality extra-virgin olive oil

2 lemons, cut in ¼-inch slices

6 cloves garlic

3 shallots, thinly sliced

2 Tbsp sea salt

5 sprigs thyme

3 bay leaves

1 tsp coriander seeds

18 oz albacore tuna loin (3 large chunks)

chilled oysters with three mignonettes

At Araxi, we love oysters. Patrick, our star shucker, opens thousands every week, all of them bought directly from our local producers. We like to serve them with several contrasting mignonettes. The berry mignonette is our most popular and the most classic. Wanda Dixon, a.k.a. The Vinegar Lady, makes fantastic fresh fruit vinegars from local British Columbia berries. Her products are available online and at fine grocers.

BERRY MIGNONETTE In a small bowl, whisk together all of the ingredients until well combined. Refrigerate for at least 30 minutes to let the flavours blend. This will keep refrigerated in an airtight container for 7 to 10 days.

CUCUMBER-BASIL MIGNONETTE Place the cucumber, vinegar, shallot, basil, salt and sugar in a blender and process at medium speed until smooth. With the motor running, slowly pour in the olive oil until the mignonette is smooth and emulsified. This will keep refrigerated in an airtight container for 2 to 3 days.

SWEET AND SOUR PLUM MIGNONETTE Place all of the ingredients in a small saucepan and bring to a boil on medium-low heat. Cook for 8 to 10 minutes, until the plums are softened, then remove from the heat and let stand for 10 minutes in a warm place.

Pour the plum mixture into a blender and process at high speed until smooth. Set a fine-mesh sieve over a bowl and strain the mignonette through it. Discard any solids. Refrigerate the sauce until well chilled, about 30 minutes. This will keep refrigerated in an airtight container for about 1 week.

TO SERVE Have ready several large platters of crushed ice. Pour each of the mignonettes into separate ramekins or sauceboats. Carefully shuck your pristine oysters and immediately place them on the ice. Arrange the ramekins (or sauceboats) on the platters and garnish with lemon wedges. Try a different mignonette on each oyster; be sure to try all 3. They are best enjoyed if you put one on each oyster instead of a combination, so as to not overwhelm your taste buds.

berry mignonette

½ cup Vinegar Lady raspberry vinegar

½ cup Vinegar Lady blackberry vinegar

1 Tbsp honey

2 medium shallots, minced

4 sprigs thyme, leaves only

cucumber-basil mignonette

1 English cucumber, peeled, seeds removed and roughly chopped

¾ cup white wine vinegar

1 large shallot, peeled and diced

10 basil leaves

2 tsp kosher salt

1 tsp granulated sugar

¾ cup extra-virgin olive oil

sweet and sour plum mignonette

7 oz fresh plums, pits removed and roughly chopped

1 cup rice wine vinegar

¼ cup granulated sugar

2½ Tbsp mirin

1 Tbsp minced fresh ginger

1 tsp kosher salt

chilled oysters

3 dozen fresh oysters, well chilled (Satori, Zen, Kusshi and Black Pearl are some of our favourites)

3 lemons, cut into wedges

geoduck clams with shaved fennel & apple dressing

Geoduck clams are plentiful in British Columbia waters and have a surprisingly sweet flavour that is very well complemented by the slightly tart Granny Smith apples. Geoduck can be hard to find sometimes, so if they are proving difficult to source, you could use cooked littleneck or Manila clams instead. And arugula or kale work well in this recipe if watercress is not in season.

APPLE DRESSING Place the apples, shallot, vinegar, mustard and sugar in a blender or food processor and process on medium speed for 2 to 3 minutes, or until smooth. With the motor running, slowly add the vegetable and olive oils until well combined. Set a fine-mesh sieve over a clean bowl and strain the apple dressing. Discard the solids. Lightly season the dressing with salt. This will keep refrigerated in an airtight container for 2 to 3 days.

GEODUCK SALAD Soak the sliced fennel in ice water for ten minutes. Place the geoduck, fennel and watercress in a large salad bowl.

TO SERVE Have ready 4 chilled plates. Drizzle the geoduck salad with the apple dressing and toss lightly to combine. Divide the salad evenly among the individual plates. Drizzle each plate with a little more dressing.

apple dressing

2 Granny Smith apples, peeled, cored and chopped

1 shallot, sliced

¼ cup maple vinegar or sherry vinegar

1 Tbsp grainy mustard

1 tsp brown sugar

⅔ cup vegetable oil

¼ cup extra-virgin olive oil

Sea salt to taste

geoduck salad

1 medium geoduck clam, cleaned, blanched and skin removed then thinly sliced

1 medium fennel bulb, thinly sliced

½ cup watercress, leaves only, washed

GRILLED OCTOPUS
"JORGE STYLE"
page 164

grilled octopus "jorge style"

MARINATED OCTOPUS Fill a large saucepan with a tight-fitting lid with lightly salted water and bring to a boil on high heat. Place the octopus in a colander in the sink and sprinkle liberally with sea salt. Using your hands, rub the octopus along the sides of the colander to remove the film from the tentacles. Rub for about 3 minutes, then rinse under cold water to remove the salt and film. Pat dry with paper towels.

Using tongs, dip the octopus into the boiling water for 30 seconds and then lift it out. Let stand for 1 minute. Dip the octopus in the boiling water for another 30 seconds, then lift it out and let stand for 1 minute. Repeat this process once more. (This step makes the octopus legs curl for a more dramatic presentation.) Next, immerse the octopus in the boiling water, and turn down the heat to a simmer. Cover the pot and cook the octopus for 45 to 50 minutes, or until a knife inserted into the thickest part of the leg comes out easily. Transfer the cooked octopus to a large bowl and allow it to cool.

Using a sharp knife, remove and discard any excess skin from the thick parts of the tentacles near the head. Return the octopus to the bowl, add the garlic, parsley, lemon juice and zest, and olive oil and toss well. Refrigerate for 1 hour or overnight.

Preheat the barbecue or an indoor grill to medium-high heat. Brush the grill with a lightly oiled rag or kitchen towel to prevent sticking, then place the marinated octopus on the grill and sear for 5 to 6 minutes. You will smell the lemon and garlic.

marinated octopus

4 to 5 lb octopus, head cleaned and ink sac removed

Sea salt to taste

2 cloves garlic, minced

2 Tbsp chopped flat-leaf parsley

Juice and zest of 2 lemons

2 Tbsp extra-virgin olive oil

1 recipe Romesco Sauce (page 221)

Jorge Muñoz Santos is a cook from Spain who worked at Araxi for four years. He now heads the kitchen at Bar Oso. This dish is his favourite way to cook octopus and it's a somewhat classic preparation. In our local waters, the octopus is fantastic and should be enjoyed frequently. Grilling really highlights its sweetness. Serve with a green salad.

Using tongs, turn the octopus over, turn down the heat to medium and cook for a further 5 to 6 minutes. Remove from the grill and let rest while you prepare the potatoes.

PAN-FRIED POTATOES In a small frying pan, heat the olive oil on medium-high heat. Add the potatoes and sauté for 6 to 8 minutes, or until lightly golden and heated through. Remove from the heat and sprinkle with the smoked paprika and sea salt to taste.

TO SERVE Spoon a generous amount of romesco sauce onto each plate. Garnish with potatoes. Using a sharp knife, cut the octopus into 3 to 4-inch pieces and serve 3 to 4 pieces per person, placing the octopus on top of the potatoes. Serve warm.

pan-fried potatoes
1 Tbsp extra-virgin olive oil

1 lb new potatoes, cut in half and boiled until tender

½ tsp smoked paprika

Sea salt to taste

crispy oyster "po' boy" tacos & salsa verde

SALSA VERDE Place all of the ingredients in a food processor and blend at high speed until smooth. Set a fine-mesh sieve over a clean bowl and strain the salsa verde through it. Discard the solids. Cover and refrigerate immediately. This can be refrigerated in an airtight container for up to 2 days. It loses its colour and flavour if stored for longer.

CRISPY OYSTERS Place the oysters in a large bowl, cover with the buttermilk and refrigerate for 30 minutes.

Place a fine-mesh sieve over a clean bowl and strain the buttermilk through it. Set aside the oysters. To the strained buttermilk, add the eggs and whisk until well combined. Place the flour in a second bowl, and in a third, separate bowl mix together the bread crumbs, Parmesan and cornmeal. Set the bowls side by side on the counter in the following order: flour, buttermilk, bread crumbs.

Working in batches of 6, dip the oysters in the flour and shake off any excess. Place the oysters in the buttermilk, coating them completely. Using a slotted spoon and shaking off any excess buttermilk, transfer the oysters to the the bread crumb mixture, rolling them with your fingers to coat the oysters evenly. Shake off any excess crumbs and set the battered oysters on a plate. Refrigerate, and repeat the process with the remaining oysters.

salsa verde

8 medium tomatillos, peeled and cut into quarters

1 avocado, pitted and peeled

1 green onion, white and green parts, sliced

1 clove garlic, peeled

Juice of 3 limes

½ green jalapeño pepper, seeds removed

2 Tbsp chopped cilantro leaves

¼ cup grapeseed oil

1 Tbsp sea salt

crispy oysters

3 dozen medium fresh oysters, shucked and juices reserved for another use

1½ cups buttermilk

3 eggs

1 cup all-purpose flour

2 cups panko bread crumbs

½ cup grated Parmesan cheese

½ cup finely ground cornmeal

6 cups vegetable oil for deep-frying

One summer, we wanted to highlight our fantastic local oysters. We took the classic "po' boy" sandwich, that cornmeal-crusted deep-fried oyster served on a soft bun, and turned it into a delicious taco. Instead of the traditional hot sauce, we used this really tasty, summery salsa verde. If you don't have any oysters, you can use lingcod, salmon or halibut. Adding different seasonal vegetables or spicy greens to your tacos is also a nice touch.

Line a plate with paper towels. In a deep fryer, wok or deep-sided saucepan, heat the vegetable oil to 340°F. Check the temperature of the oil using a deep-fat thermometer. Once the oil is hot enough, add the oysters in batches of 12 and cook for about 90 seconds, or until lightly golden brown. Using a slotted spoon, transfer the oysters to the lined plate to drain. Fry the remaining oysters. Set the oysters in a warm place while you assemble the tacos.

"PO' BOY" TACOS Arrange the tortillas on a clean work surface. Divide the carrots and cabbage evenly among the tortillas, placing them down the centre. Drizzle with salsa verde. Place 3 oysters on each tortilla, drizzle with sour cream and top with a sprig of cilantro.

TO SERVE Place 2 tacos on each plate and serve immediately with wedges of lime.

"po' boy" tacos

12 corn or flour tortillas, each 8 inches in diameter, warmed

2 medium carrots, peeled and coarsely grated

½ head of firm green cabbage, rinsed and shredded

1 recipe Salsa Verde (see opposite)

12 sprigs cilantro

1 cup sour cream

3 limes, cut into wedges

dungeness crab cakes with corn salsa

CORN SALSA Using a sharp knife, cut the corn kernels off the cobs (see page 74 for a handy method). Place the kernels in a bowl and discard the cobs (or reserve them for another use).

Bring a medium pot of lightly salted water to a boil on high heat. Add the corn kernels and cook for 5 minutes. Drain the corn, place it in a large bowl and set it aside to cool.

To the bowl of corn, add the tomatoes, green onions, jalapeño, bell pepper and cilantro and toss well to combine.

Heat the olive oil in a small saucepan on medium heat. Once the oil is hot, add the cumin and lightly toast in the oil for 30 seconds. Stir in the tomato paste and cook for a further 2 minutes. Remove from the heat and whisk in the vinegar and sugar. Pour this cumin-tomato mixture over the corn and mix thoroughly. Season with salt and refrigerate until needed. This will keep refrigerated in an airtight container for 3 days.

PEACH PURÉE Combine all ingredients in a small saucepan. Place on medium-low heat and bring to a simmer. Cover the pot with a lid and cook for approximately 10-12 minutes, or until peaches are soft and the skins are starting to fall off. Remove from the heat and place in a blender, processing on high until smooth. Press the purée through a fine strainer and place, uncovered, in a bowl in the fridge until cool.

corn salsa

3 ears of fresh corn, husks removed

3 Roma tomatoes, peeled and diced

2 green onions, white and green parts, finely chopped

1 jalapeño pepper, seeds removed, finely chopped

1 red bell pepper, diced

2 Tbsp chopped cilantro

½ cup extra-virgin olive oil

2 tsp ground cumin

2 Tbsp tomato paste

¼ cup rice vinegar

1 Tbsp granulated sugar

Sea salt to taste

peach purée

3 ripe peaches, halved, pits removed and cut into ½-inch chunks

2 Tbsp rice vinegar

1 Tbsp sugar

1 pinch sea salt

½ cup water

This recipe is my take on crab cakes, which I like moist and not too firm. The salsa is not only fantastic with this dish, it is also perfect over grilled meats or fish or even scattered in a salad. A drizzle of fresh peach purée to finish provides an added twist.

CRAB CAKES In a large chilled bowl, combine the crabmeat, fine bread crumbs, green onion, cilantro and ginger with the yuzu mayonnaise and lime juice and zest. Season lightly with salt and white pepper, then mix thoroughly but gently to avoid breaking up the crabmeat too much. Using your hands, divide the crab mixture into 8 evenly sized balls and refrigerate until ready to bread.

Just before you're ready to serve, heat the canola (or vegetable) oil in a deep fryer, wok or deep saucepan to 330°F.

While the oil is heating up, combine the eggs and the milk in a small bowl and whisk to combine thoroughly. Place the flour in a second bowl, and the panko bread crumbs in a third, separate bowl.

Remove the crab mixture from the fridge and, using your hands, lightly press each of the balls into a puck shape so the cakes will cook evenly. One at a time, first dip the cakes into the flour and shake off any excess, then place them in the egg mixture and, lastly, in the bread crumbs. You can refrigerate the crab cakes until you are ready to cook them.

Line a plate with paper towels and place it in a warm place. Use a deep-fat thermometer to test the temperature of the oil. When it is hot enough, quickly drop 3 of the crab cakes into the hot oil, frying them until lightly golden and crispy, about 3 minutes. Using a slotted spoon, transfer the crab cakes to the paper towels to drain. Repeat with the remaining crab cakes, cooking them in batches of 2 or 3 until they are all cooked.

TO SERVE Arrange the cooked crab cakes on a serving platter, garnish them with the corn salsa and drizzle with the Peach Purée, if using. Serve immediately.

crab cakes

2 lb Dungeness crabmeat, picked of shells or cartilage

½ cup fine dried bread crumbs

1 large green onion, white and green parts, finely chopped

1 Tbsp chopped cilantro

1 Tbsp minced fresh ginger

½ cup Yuzu Mayonnaise (page 219)

Juice and zest of 1 lime

Sea salt and cracked white pepper to taste

4 cups canola or vegetable oil

2 eggs

¾ cup whole milk

1 cup all-purpose flour

2 cups panko bread crumbs

1 recipe Peach Purée, optional (see opposite)

DUNGENESS
CRAB CAKES
WITH CORN SALSA
page 168

SEARED
WILD SCALLOPS
WITH CAULIFLOWER
TEMPURA
page 172

171

seared wild scallops with cauliflower tempura

RAISIN VINAIGRETTE In a small bowl, whisk together all of the ingredients except the raisins and salt. Add a pinch of sea salt and adjust the seasoning if needed. Add the raisins. This will keep refrigerated in an airtight container for up to 5 days.

CAULIFLOWER TEMPURA Have ready a large bowl of ice water. Fill a medium saucepan with lightly salted water and bring to a boil on high heat. Add the cauliflower and cook for 3 minutes. Using a slotted spoon, transfer the cauliflower to the bowl of ice water to stop the cooking. Allow it to cool completely, drain and set aside.

Combine the egg yolks and sparkling water in a stainless steel bowl and mix lightly. Gently stir in the flour with a fork until just combined (do not overmix or the coating will become heavy). Refrigerate this tempura batter.

In a deep fryer, wok or deep saucepan, heat the vegetable oil to 340°F while you sear the scallops.

SEARED SCALLOPS Heat the olive oil in a sauté pan on medium heat (the oil should not be heated for too long or it will burn).

In a small bowl, combine the salt and curry powder until well mixed. Working quickly, lightly sprinkle this over both sides of the scallops. Place the scallops in the sauté pan and cook until golden brown on both sides, 1 to 2 minutes per side depending upon the thickness of the scallops. Transfer to a plate and set in a warm place.

raisin vinaigrette

¾ cup grapeseed oil

¼ cup sherry vinegar

2 Tbsp maple syrup

2 tsp grainy Dijon mustard

½ tsp ground cumin

Pinch of sea salt

½ cup golden raisins, soaked in warm water until softened and then drained

cauliflower tempura

2 cups cauliflower florets

5 cups vegetable oil for frying

2 egg yolks

2 cups sparkling water

2 cups all-purpose flour, sifted

½ tsp Espelette chili powder

½ tsp salt

seared scallops

2 Tbsp extra-virgin olive oil

1 Tbsp sea salt

¼ tsp curry powder (we use a mild Madras)

12 fresh scallops, cleaned and adductor muscle removed

Being close to the ocean, we are blessed with access to delicious fresh seafood—especially scallops. I find that searing scallops highlights their natural sweetness and adding raisins only further accents that flavour. Espelette pepper is a chili blend from France that can be found in the spice aisle of fine grocers and is lightly spicy and very flavourful.

FINISH TEMPURA As soon as you have set the scallops in a warm place, remove the tempura batter from the fridge and add the cauliflower to it, stirring the florets gently until they are well coated.

Line a plate with paper towels. Check the temperature of the oil using a deep-fat thermometer. Once the oil is hot enough, cook the cauliflower in 3 batches. Using tongs, place ⅓ of the battered cauliflower florets in the deep fryer (or wok or saucepan) and cook until light golden and crispy, about 2 minutes per batch. Transfer the cooked cauliflower to the paper towels to drain. Cook the remaining cauliflower in 2 batches. Lightly season the tempura with the Espelette pepper and salt.

TO SERVE Arrange 3 scallops on each plate and drizzle them with the raisin vinaigrette. Top the scallops with several pieces of cauliflower tempura and serve immediately.

OYSTERS BAKED
IN SEAWEED
WITH FONDUTO
page 176

SERVES
4 TO 6
AS PART
OF AN
ENTRÉE
PLATTER

oysters baked in seaweed with fonduto

I first cooked this dish on a beach in Tofino, on the west coast of Vancouver Island. It's easy to make at home. Seaweed, like many vegetables, comes in various sizes, textures and shapes. For this recipe, we like the firmness and size of bull kelp, alaria or kombu. We use a medium to large roasting oyster (which is considerably larger than the shucking kind) and top it with a fonduto, an Italian cheese sauce.

Place the cream, garlic, bay leaves and lemon thyme in a medium saucepan and bring them to a boil on medium-high heat. Turn off the heat and let stand for 10 minutes.

In a medium bowl, combine the 3 cheeses. Pour the warm cream over top, stirring until the cheese has melted and is smooth and well combined. Set a fine-mesh sieve over a small saucepan and strain the fonduto through it. Discard any solids. Cover the pot and place it in a warm place.

Set the oven rack in the middle of the oven. Preheat the oven to 400°F. Arrange a thin layer of seaweed on a baking tray, place the oysters on top and cover with the remaining seaweed. Set the lemon halves, cut side down, around the tray and then bake for 20 minutes.

Remove the baking tray from the oven. The seaweed should be very hot and the lemons soft. Return the baking tray to the oven for 5 more minutes while you warm the fonduto.

TO SERVE Have ready a large serving platter. Bring the cheese mixture to a simmer on low heat. Remove the baking tray from the oven and, using tongs, carefully pull the oysters out of the seaweed and place them in a bowl. Using a kitchen towel to hold the oysters, gently insert an oyster knife (or a flat screwdriver) into the hinge where the two sides of the shell meet. Twist the knife and pop the top shell off, exposing the baked oyster. With a knife, carefully loosen the oyster from the bottom part of the shell. Discard the top shell and set the oyster, in its bottom shell, on the serving platter. Work quickly! Squeeze the juice from the warm lemons over the oysters and top each one with a spoonful of fonduto. Enjoy!

2 cups whipping cream

1 clove garlic, sliced

2 bay leaves

2 sprigs lemon thyme

¼ cup goat cheese

½ cup grated Pecorino cheese

½ cup grated Gruyère cheese

2 to 3 lb seaweed, rinsed

12 large oysters, each with a shell 5 to 6 inches long

6 lemons, cut in half

SERVES
4 TO 6
AS A
BEACH
OR PATIO
ENTRÉE

scallops in the shell with sea urchin butter

This is a great dish for a party, because it never fails to impress. Sea urchins and scallops grow together, so they go together. Sea urchin roe can be purchased at Japanese grocers or from your local fishmonger. It is best at certain times of the year, mainly spring and winter when the waters are cold, but enjoy it whenever possible. You can freeze the sea urchin butter for up to a week.

Have ready an 11 × 18-inch piece of parchment paper or plastic wrap. Place the butter in a large bowl. Using a spatula, spread the butter around the bowl to further soften it. Fold in the sea urchin roe, chives, lemon zest and white pepper; mix thoroughly and gently until well combined.

Place the parchment paper (or plastic wrap) on a clean work surface. Scoop the sea urchin butter into a horizontal line down the middle of the sheet. Fold the edge of the sheet closest to you over the butter, then continue rolling the paper (or plastic wrap), tightly encasing the butter and forming a log shape. Twist the ends of the roll to seal them and place this flavoured butter in the fridge. This will keep refrigerated for 2 days or frozen for 1 week.

To prepare the scallops, use a sharp knife to loosen the meat from the shell. Remove and discard the stomach and connective tissue but reserve the shells. Replace each scallop in its shell, set them on a plate and refrigerate while you prepare the baking tray.

Preheat the oven to 425°F. To hold the scallops upright and as level as possible while cooking, line a baking tray with aluminum foil, crimping it like you would to make a fan, to cup the shells. Arrange the scallops in their shells on the tray.

Unwrap the chilled butter and cut it into ¼-inch slices. Put a slice of butter on top of each scallop and bake the scallops for 6 minutes. Turn the tray 180 degrees and cook the scallops for a further 2 minutes. The scallops should be firm, white and slightly translucent.

TO SERVE Arrange the scallops in the shell on a serving platter. Sprinkle each one with a small pinch of sea salt and serve immediately.

1¼ cups unsalted butter, softened
2 oz sea urchin roe
1 Tbsp chopped chives
Zest of 1 lemon
½ tsp cracked white pepper
12 large fresh scallops, in the shell

roasted sablefish tail on root vegetables

Rinse the sablefish under cold running water and pat it dry with paper towels. Place the fish on a plate. Using a very sharp knife, score the fish on both sides of its body at 2-inch intervals, about ⅛ inch deep. Cover and refrigerate the sablefish.

Preheat the oven to 375°F. Line a baking sheet with parchment paper. Bring a large pot of lightly salted water to a boil on high heat. Add the potatoes and cook for 6 to 8 minutes, or until they are about half cooked. Use a knife to cut one in half to check. Drain the potatoes, and while they are still warm, arrange them on the lined baking sheet. Add the onions, sunchokes, parsnips, carrots, garlic and bay leaves. Drizzle with 2 Tbsp of the olive oil and season with 1 tsp of the salt and a large pinch of cracked black pepper. Using your hands, gently and thoroughly mix the vegetables and mound them down the centre of the tray. Bake for 5 minutes.

While the vegetables are roasting, remove the sablefish from the fridge and place it on a cutting board. Brush the fish with the remaining olive oil and season generously with the remaining salt and pepper. Remove the tray of roasted vegetables from the oven, place the fish on top and arrange the lemon halves around the fish. Return to the oven and roast for 20 minutes.

Tail half of a sablefish, 4 to 5 lb, skin on but scaled

2 lb new potatoes, cut in half

18 small cipollini onions, peeled

12 medium sunchokes, washed and halved lengthwise

4 medium parsnips, peeled and cut in 3-inch-long and ½-inch-wide batons

3 medium carrots, peeled and cut in 3-inch-long and ½-inch-wide batons

1 head of garlic, split lengthwise

3 bay leaves

3 Tbsp extra-virgin olive oil

2 tsp sea salt

Cracked black pepper to taste

2 lemons, cut in half

Sablefish, or black cod as it is commonly known, does very well when roasted. It retains its moisture and doesn't dry out like other fish, especially with the bones in. We use the tail end of the fish for this dish, leaving the fattier front fillets for other preparations. This dish works with lingcod or other moist white fish as well. Try it. You'll like it.

After 20 minutes, check on the fish and the root vegetables. The fish should be browning and the vegetables should be softening. Cook for a further 10 minutes. To test for doneness, insert the tip of a knife into the wider end of the fish, close to the centre bone. Press the knife up to reveal the flesh. The meat should be white, flaky and slightly translucent. Remove the tray from the oven.

TO SERVE Gently lift the fish off the vegetables and onto a cutting board. Transfer the vegetables onto a serving platter. Insert your knife at the top of the fish along the centre bone and cut down to the end of the tail. Repeat this cut along the belly part of the fish. Using a spatula, lift up the top fillet of the fish and place it on the vegetables. Use a fork or the tip of a knife to pull out and discard the backbone of the fish. Set the bottom fillet of the fish on the platter with the vegetables. Garnish with the warm lemons and serve. Invite your guests to squeeze the lemons over their individual servings to moisten the fish.

sunshine coast sturgeon & caviar with beet salsa

Target Marine Hatcheries in West Sechelt on the Sunshine Coast produce beautiful natural, organic and sustainable Northern Divine caviar and white sturgeon fillets and loins. We've served this dish at several wine dinners, and people are always amazed at the meatiness of the sturgeon and the delicacy of the caviar, both sourced from the same fish.

BEET SALSA AND CAVIAR In a large bowl, combine the beets, shallot, ginger, orange juice and zest, olive oil and maple (or apple) vinegar. Toss gently and season lightly with salt and pepper. Cover and refrigerate until needed.

ROASTED STURGEON Preheat the oven to 375°F. In an ovenproof sauté pan, heat the olive oil on medium heat. Season the sturgeon steaks with the salt and pepper, add them to the pan with the thyme and cook for 2 to 3 minutes, until golden. Place the pan in the oven and cook for a further 5 minutes.

Return the pan to the stove on medium heat. Turn the sturgeon and add the butter to the pan. As the butter melts, use a spoon to baste the fish evenly for 1 minute. Transfer the sturgeon steaks to individual plates.

TO SERVE Spoon some of the beet salsa over and around the fish on each plate. Drizzle the pan juices over the fish. Top each serving with a dab of the caviar and sprinkle with chives.

beet salsa and caviar

1 cup finely diced roasted red beets

1 small shallot, finely minced

1 tsp grated fresh ginger

Juice and zest of 1 orange

3 Tbsp extra-virgin olive oil

2 Tbsp maple or apple vinegar

Sea salt and ground black pepper to taste

1 oz Northern Divine sturgeon caviar, for garnish

1 tsp chopped fresh chives, for garnish

roasted sturgeon

2 Tbsp extra-virgin olive oil

4 sturgeon steaks, each 6 oz

Sea salt and cracked black pepper to taste

2 sprigs thyme

2 Tbsp unsalted butter

HAVING SURVIVED two ice ages, the local Fraser River white sturgeon are among the oldest species of fish in the world, but their wild stocks are threatened by overfishing. Since 2000, Target Marine Hatcheries near Sechelt on the Sunshine Coast has been raising these fish in large outdoor, land-based tanks fed by a mountain creek and several natural aquifers. Today they are considered sustainable and are recommended by the Vancouver Aquarium's Ocean Wise program. Chef James Walt buys the whole fish as well as the eggs harvested from those fish, which are extracted, lightly salted, packed into cans and sold as Northern Divine Caviar. The buttery, nutty, slightly salty flavour of this certified organic caviar pairs perfectly with chilled Schramm vodka or Champagne, and is a perfect complement to the restaurant's signature sturgeon dish (page 181).

araxi | GOING TO THE SOURCE

THE MANY THOUSANDS of oysters that are shucked every week at Araxi's busy Oyster Bar are sourced directly from three chief suppliers: Sawmill Bay Shellfish Company, which farms the chilly waters off Read Island in the Salish Sea's Discovery group of islands; Out Landish Shellfish Guild, a group of eight family-run farms operating off Quadra, Read and Cortes Islands; and Hollie Wood Oysters, a small Comox Valley company that grows oysters in the pristine waters off Denman Island. "The oyster is the grape of the sea," says Chef Walt. "It has its own terroir. The part of the ocean it came from is literally trapped inside. To me, nothing tastes like BC more than a fresh, raw oyster."

MOST OF ARAXI'S meats come from Two Rivers, a Sea-to-Sky company that partners with local farms that specialize in humanely raised local, organic and chemical-free meats like beef, pork, lamb, Blue Foot chicken and a variety of game birds. The duck from Yarrow Meadows in the Fraser Valley, for example, is a mainstay on Araxi's menus. The leg meat is confited for terrines; the liver can anchor a parfait or hide in gougères; and the breast is often pan-roasted and served with polenta. Before Margot and Jason Pleym launched Two Rivers in 2007 (based on an idea they hatched while living in a yellow school bus next to the Kicking Horse River), local chefs were hard-pressed to find meats of estimable provenance in the volumes required by a busy restaurant. "What Two Rivers has done for the restaurant and retail meat supply across the Lower Mainland and up the Sea-to-Sky is revolutionary," says Chef Walt.

araxi
après
fondue

About five years ago we started to offer this fondue from 3:00 p.m. each day, before we open the restaurant for dinner. It didn't take long for this mix of ski resort, cold weather and warm, cheesy goodness to take off. Who knew it would become so popular? This very classic recipe is only as good as its ingredients, so use the very best cheese and wine you can find.

Set up your fondue base burner with fuel and prepare the dipping ingredients. Arrange the lightly toasted bread cubes and the sausage (or ham) on a serving platter. Place the gherkins (or pickles) and apple slices in separate small bowls.

Rub the the inside of the fondue pot with the garlic, then discard both halves. Place the pot on the stove (not the fondue base) on medium heat, add the white wine and bring it to a boil. Turn down the heat to a simmer. Using a whisk, mix the cheeses into the wine, a handful at a time, whisking slowly as the cheese melts. The mixture will start to thicken. Once all of the cheese has been added, turn down the heat to low.

In a small bowl, mix the cornstarch with the kirsch, stirring until they are well mixed. Whisking continuously, add the cornstarch mixture to the fondue in a steady stream and cook for 3 to 4 minutes, until the fondue is thickened and smooth and has reached a simmer. Remove the pot from the heat and dip a piece of bread into the fondue to check the seasoning. Add a little sea salt if necessary, and finish with a sprinkle of freshly grated nutmeg.

Place the fondue burner in the middle of the table, light it and place the fondue pot on top. Adjust the heat until the cheese is slightly bubbling. Pass around plates and fondue forks and allow guests to help themselves to the bread, sausage, gherkins and apple slices.

4 cups good-quality crusty bread, cut in 1½-inch cubes and lightly toasted

10 oz cooked sausage or cooked ham, cut in ¼-inch slices or cubes

½ cup gherkins or assorted pickles, cut in half

1 Granny Smith apple, skin on, sliced

1 clove garlic, cut in half

2¾ cups white wine (we use Grüner Veltliner or Riesling)

15 oz Gruyère cheese, grated

8 oz Emmenthal cheese, grated

2½ Tbsp cornstarch

3 oz kirsch

Sea salt to taste

Freshly grated nutmeg

seared duck breasts with fresh horseradish & sesame

DUCK BRINE Preheat the oven to 350°F. Place the water, sugar and kosher and pink salts in a small saucepan on low heat until the solids have just dissolved. Remove from the heat and set aside.

Set the coriander seeds, peppercorns, fennel seeds, cloves, star anise and cinnamon stick on a baking tray and toast in the oven for 5 to 6 minutes, or until you can clearly smell the spices. Remove the spices from the oven and add them to the cooling brine. Stir in the rosemary and thyme, cover and refrigerate for at least 12 hours. Strain the brine through a fine-mesh sieve into a container large enough to hold the duck breasts in a single layer. Discard the solids.

SEARED DUCK BREASTS To the container of strained brine, add the duck breasts, cover and refrigerate for 12 to 18 hours.

Preheat the oven to 350°F. Heat an ovenproof nonstick sauté pan on medium heat. Remove the duck breasts from the brine and pat them dry with paper towels. Place the duck breasts, skin side down, in the dry sauté pan (if the pan is too small for all 6 duck breasts, cook them 3 at a time). Once the duck breasts start to render their juices and the skins begin to shrink and turn golden, about 4 minutes, carefully pour off the liquid. Turn the duck breasts over and cook for about 1 minute to seal the flesh side.

duck brine

4 cups water

2 Tbsp granulated sugar

4 to 5 tsp kosher salt

1 tsp pink salt (salt nitrate)

2 Tbsp coriander seeds

1 Tbsp black peppercorns

1 Tbsp fennel seeds

4 whole cloves

4 star anise pods

1 cinnamon stick

1 sprig rosemary

1 sprig thyme

seared duck breasts

1 recipe Duck Brine (see above)

6 duck breasts, each 8 to 9 oz, cleaned of sinew and skin lightly scored

3 cups fresh baby spinach leaves

1 recipe Sesame-soy Vinaigrette (page 219)

1 Tbsp toasted sesame seeds

finely diced red radish, for garnish

Thinly sliced daikon or watermelon radish, for garnish

The brine, which is really the foundation of this dish, is based on a recipe from a dear friend, Owen Lightly: a great chef who passed on too soon. Start this dish two days before you plan to serve it so you have time to make the brine and steep the duck breasts in it. It adds great flavour and keeps the duck nice and moist. Use local duck when you can. We buy ours from Yarrow Meadows in the Fraser Valley.

If the pan is big enough to hold all of the duck breasts at once, place it in the oven for 8 to 10 minutes. If not, sear all of the breasts, then transfer all 6 to a large ovenproof dish and place it in the oven for 8 to 10 minutes. To check the duck for doneness, insert a sharp knife into the centre of the thickest duck breast. When you pull the knife out, the tip should just be warm. The duck should be medium rare to medium. Use an instant-read meat thermometer to double-check the temperature.

Transfer the duck to a plate, pour the cooking juices over the breasts, loosely cover with aluminum foil and let rest in a warm place for about 10 minutes.

TO SERVE In a bowl, toss the spinach leaves with 2 Tbsp of the vinaigrette until lightly coated. Mound the spinach in the centre of a serving platter and arrange the duck breasts around it. Drizzle the duck with more vinaigrette (you won't need it all) and sprinkle with the toasted sesame seeds. Garnish with the thinly sliced daikon or watermelon radish.

SEARED DUCK
BREASTS WITH
FRESH HORSERADISH
& SESAME
page 186

MARK'S RABBIT
SAUSAGE
page 190

mark's rabbit sausage

Spread the rabbit, pork shoulder cubes and back fat on a baking tray and place in the freezer for 5 to 10 minutes, until partially frozen. Using a stand mixer fitted with a grinder attachment and a ⅜-inch die, grind the meat into a large bowl, cover it and refrigerate until chilled, about 45 minutes.

To the bowl of chilled ground meat, add the fennel and coriander seeds, sugar, pepper, chili flakes, garlic powder, and pink and kosher salts and mix thoroughly. Grind the meat once more using the same size die and return it to the fridge to chill once again, about 45 minutes to 1 hour.

Fit your stand mixer with the paddle attachment. Place the sausage mixture in the bowl of your mixer. With the motor running at low to medium speed, add the water, vinegar, pistachios, parsley and basil and mix until well incorporated. Cover and return to the fridge for 30 minutes.

Using a sausage stuffer or a piping bag fitted with a wide tip, feed the hog casing onto the nozzle. When you reach the end of the casing, tie a knot so the sausage filling will stay in place when pushed into the casing. Scoop the filling into the stuffer or piping bag and proceed to fill the casing until you have used all of the meat. Carefully remove the filled sausage from the stuffer (or piping bag). If you can, twist the long coil into 5 to 6-inch lengths. Starting at the knotted end, pinch a section at the 5 to 6-inch point to move the meat out of the way slightly and then twist the casing 2 to 3 times. When twisting the sausages, twist the first clockwise and then the next counterclockwise, and so on until completed.

1½ lb boneless rabbit meat, cut in ½-inch cubes

1½ lb pork shoulder, cut in ½-inch cubes

8 oz pork back fat, cut in ¼-inch cubes

1 Tbsp fennel seeds

½ Tbsp coriander seeds

1 Tbsp granulated sugar

1 tsp ground black pepper

½ tsp chili flakes

½ tsp garlic powder

¼ tsp pink salt (salt nitrate) (optional)

1 oz kosher salt (about 3 Tbsp)

½ cup ice water

¼ cup red wine vinegar

¼ cup toasted pistachios

½ cup chopped flat-leaf parsley

⅓ cup chopped fresh basil

3 to 4 feet hog casings, soaked in water

2 Tbsp extra-virgin olive oil

Making sausages is surprisingly easy. You just need a grinding attachment for your stand mixer or food processor and you can buy hog casings from your butcher. This tasty recipe was developed by Araxi's executive sous chef, Mark McLoughlin, and uses rabbit, which we serve plenty of at the restaurant. It makes enough for a large picnic-style dinner, or you can freeze the sausages for up to a month, thawing them in the fridge for three to four days before you cook them. I like to eat this sausage with a green salad, good mustard and some house-made pickles.

Finish with a final knot. (You should have 10 to 12 large sausage links.) We also like to leave the coil whole for a really fun presentation or for a large group.

Preheat the oven to 375°F. Lightly grease a roasting pan or baking tray with ½ of the olive oil. Arrange the sausage links or whole coil on the pan (or tray) and drizzle it with the remaining oil. Roast for about 20 minutes or until an instant-read thermometer inserted into the middle of the thickest part of the sausage reaches 155°F. Remove from the oven and let rest for 10 minutes in a warm place.

TO SERVE Cut between the sausage links with a sharp knife or scissors. Transfer the individual sausages (or the entire coil) to a platter. Serve with a sharp knife.

"stretch the steak" tartine with aged provolone

When you want to buy three steaks and feed six people, this is the perfect recipe. And everything can be cooked on the barbecue. A tartine is an open-faced sandwich, and, in this case, we grill the bread to highlight the flavour of the steak. Try this recipe with lamb, chicken or even grilled fish instead of beef.

Preheat the barbecue or an indoor grill to medium-high heat. Rub the steaks with 1 Tbsp of the olive oil. Season them evenly with all of the black pepper and a pinch of sea salt. Place the steaks on the hot grill and cook for 2 minutes. Turn them 90 degrees to create the lovely grill marks that everybody likes and cook for a further 2 minutes. Turn the steaks over and cook them for 2 minutes, then turn them 90 degrees and cook for 2 minutes more. Transfer the cooked steaks to a plate and let them rest in a warm place for 8 minutes.

While the steaks are resting, drizzle 2 Tbsp of the remaining olive oil evenly over both sides of the bread slices. Place them on the grill for 45 seconds to 1 minute per side, or until lightly charred and golden brown. Remove the bread from the grill and spread one side of each slice with some of the romesco sauce. Arrange the bread slices on a baking tray.

Preheat a broiler on high. Cut the steaks into slices ¼ inch thick (each steak should yield 8 to 10 slices, depending upon its thickness). Arrange 4 to 5 slices of steak on each piece of bread and cover with 1 or 2 slices of the provolone cheese. Place the bread under the broiler just until the cheese starts to melt. Set the steak tartines on a serving platter.

TO SERVE In a bowl, toss the arugula leaves with the remaining 1 Tbsp olive oil. Top the tartines with the arugula and garnish with more shaved provolone, if desired. Serve immediately.

3 well-marbled sirloin steaks, each 10 oz

4 Tbsp extra-virgin olive oil

1 Tbsp cracked black pepper

Pinch of sea salt

6 slices of rustic bread, each 6 to 7 inches long and ½ inch thick

6 Tbsp Romesco Sauce (page 221)

6 to 8 slices aged provolone, each ⅛ inch thick

2 cups arugula leaves

fresh bacon with carrots & mustard vinaigrette

FRESH BACON Pat dry the pork belly with paper towels and place it on a clean work surface. Using a sharp knife, gently score the skin, less than ⅛ inch deep, in a crosshatch pattern. Combine all of the remaining ingredients in a bowl and mix thoroughly.

Have ready a resealable plastic bag large enough to hold the pork belly or cut a 12 × 18-inch piece of plastic wrap. Place the pork on a baking tray and, using your hands, rub the belly with all of the spice mixture. Transfer the pork to the plastic bag or set it on the plastic wrap. Add all of the extra spice mix to the bag or sprinkle it over the plastic wrap. Tightly seal the plastic bag or enclose the pork belly completely in the plastic wrap. Refrigerate the pork belly for 1 week, turning it once a day.

After 1 week, unwrap the pork belly and rinse it thoroughly under cold running water. Pat dry the pork belly with paper towels, place it in a large bowl and refrigerate, uncovered, overnight. (You could smoke the pork at this point, but we do not for this recipe.)

Preheat the oven to 200°F. Set a roasting rack on top of a baking tray and place the pork belly on top. Cook the pork belly, uncovered, for 2½ to 3 hours or until an instant-read thermometer inserted in the centre of the meat reaches 150°F. Remove the pork belly from the oven and let it rest, still uncovered, in a warm place while you prepare the carrots and vinaigrette. The bacon will keep refrigerated for 4 to 5 days.

fresh bacon

5 lb fresh pork belly, skin on
1 cup brown sugar, packed
½ cup kosher salt
¼ cup maple syrup
1 clove garlic, minced
1 tsp pink salt (salt nitrate)
1 tsp coriander seeds
1 tsp ground black pepper
1 tsp fennel seeds
1 tsp fresh thyme leaves
½ tsp ground cinnamon

Who doesn't like bacon? You have to be patient with this recipe, as it takes a week or so to make, but it's a great process for home cooks to learn. In days gone by we all made our food from scratch. Pork bellies are readily available nowadays. As always, look for locally raised, hormone-free pork when possible. The finished product can be grilled for sandwiches or burgers or served alongside fried eggs and hashbrowns. Classic!

MUSTARD VINAIGRETTE Combine all of the ingredients, except the salt, in a bowl and whisk until smooth. Add sea salt, if necessary. Refrigerate until needed. This will keep refrigerated in an airtight container for 7 days.

SAUTÉED CARROTS In a sauté pan that will just hold the carrots, heat the olive oil on medium-low heat. Add all of the carrots, then toss with the sugar, white pepper and salt. Add all of the hot water, cover the pot and cook for 5 to 6 minutes, until the carrots have softened. Remove the lid and cook for a further 2 to 3 minutes, until the liquid has evaporated and the carrots are soft. Remove from the heat.

TO SERVE Slice the fresh bacon into 2-inch-thick pieces. Arrange the bacon slices on a large platter, garnish with the sautéed carrots and drizzle with the vinaigrette.

mustard vinaigrette

½ cup grapeseed or canola oil
⅓ cup grainy mustard
⅓ cup good-quality honey
2 Tbsp red wine vinegar
Pinch of sea salt (optional)

sautéed carrots

1 Tbsp extra-virgin olive oil
2 bunches baby carrots, peeled and cut into 18 to 20 pieces
1 tsp granulated sugar
¼ tsp ground white pepper
Large pinch of sea salt
¼ cup hot water

FRESH BACON WITH
CARROTS & MUSTARD
VINAIGRETTE
page 194

SLOW-COOKED
BEEF CHEEKS
IN PORT WINE
page 198

slow-cooked beef cheeks in port wine

SLOW-COOKED BEEF CHEEKS Preheat the oven to 325°F. In an oven-proof braising dish fitted with a lid, heat 2 Tbsp of the canola (or grapeseed) oil on medium heat. Season the beef cheeks on both sides with salt and pepper. Working in 2 batches, sear the beef cheeks on all sides until golden brown, 4 to 5 minutes per batch. When you have seared all the beef cheeks, pour off the fat and wipe the dish clean. Set aside the beef cheeks on a large plate.

Add the remaining 2 Tbsp of canola (or grapeseed) oil to the braising dish and heat again on medium heat. Add the shallots, garlic, carrots, celery and star anise and cook until the vegetables have coloured and softened, 8 to 10 minutes. Stir in the tomato paste and cook for 2 to 3 minutes, then pour in the port and cook for a further 8 to 10 minutes, or until the wine has reduced by half. Gently stir in the beef cheeks and bay leaves, cover with the veal (or chicken) stock and bring to a boil. As soon as the mixture comes to a boil, cover the dish with its lid and place it in the oven for 2½ to 3 hours, or until the cheeks are very tender.

Using a slotted spoon, transfer the beef cheeks to a plate and set them aside in a warm place. Strain the braising liquid through a very fine mesh sieve or a colander lined with cheesecloth into a clean pot. Use a spoon to skim off and discard any fatty juices from the top, then set the pot on medium-low heat. Cook until the juices have reduced to a sauce-like consistency, 20 to 25 minutes. Return the beef cheeks to the pot, stir well until they are warmed through and cover until needed. They can be refrigerated in an airtight container overnight.

slow-cooked beef cheeks

4 Tbsp canola oil or grapeseed oil

8 beef cheeks, each 6 to 7 oz, cleaned of sinew and connective tissue

Sea salt and ground black pepper to taste

6 large shallots, cut in half

4 cloves garlic

2 medium carrots, peeled and cut into quarters

2 stalks celery, cut into quarters

1 star anise

2 Tbsp tomato paste

1 bottle (750 mL/3 cups) ruby port wine

2 bay leaves

10 cups Veal Stock (page 220) or chicken stock

This is a luscious, melt-in-your-mouth dish that I promise you'll never forget. Beef cheeks contain a good amount of gelatin, which, combined with the slow cooking, creates an amazing sauce. Ask your butcher to source beef cheeks for you, or purchase them through fine meat companies like Two Rivers in North Vancouver or Trimpac Meats in Vancouver. Serve this dish with roasted beets or sautéed carrots.

POMME PURÉE Place the potatoes and a large pinch of salt in a large saucepan. Cover the potatoes with water and bring the pot to a boil on high heat. Turn down the heat to medium-low and let the potatoes simmer until they are fork-tender, 15 to 20 minutes. Drain the potatoes into a colander. Rinse out the pot with warm water to get rid of any excess starch. Pass the potatoes through a potato ricer and into the pot.

In a small pot, heat the cream and butter on low heat until the butter has melted. Using a spatula or a whisk, mix the cream mixture into the potatoes. Season with sea salt.

TO SERVE Place the pot of beef cheeks on medium-low heat and bring them to a simmer. In the centre of each plate, place a spoonful of the pomme purée. Top each serving with a beef cheek and garnish with 2 spoonfuls of the sauce in the pot. Serve very hot.

pomme purée
3 lb Yukon Gold or Kennebec potatoes, peeled and cut into 2-inch pieces
Sea salt to taste
1 cup whipping cream
¼ cup unsalted butter

braised lamb shanks with carrot purée

BRAISED LAMB SHANKS Preheat the oven to 325°F. Season the lamb shanks generously with salt and pepper. In a Dutch oven or a casserole dish on medium heat, warm 2 Tbsp of the olive oil in the pan and then add the lamb shanks. Rotate the shanks to brown them evenly on all sides, 7 to 8 minutes. Transfer the browned shanks to a plate.

Add the remaining 2 Tbsp olive oil to the Dutch oven or casserole dish along with the onion, carrot, celery and garlic. Season lightly with salt and pepper and cook until the vegetables have softened, 6 to 8 minutes. Stir in the tomato paste and cook for a further 2 minutes. Pour in the wine and cook until reduced by about half and lightly thickened, 8 to 10 minutes. Add the bay leaves and rosemary with the veal (or chicken) stock and bring to a boil. Return the shanks to the pot, cover and cook in the centre of the oven for 1¾ hours. The shanks should be almost falling off the bone. Return them to the oven if you think they require more cooking. Gently transfer the cooked shanks to a plate.

Strain the braising liquid through a fine-mesh sieve or a colander lined with cheesecloth into another saucepan. Discard any solids. Using a spoon, skim and discard any excess fat from the top of the liquid, then cook on medium-low heat until the liquid is slightly thickened and reduced to a sauce consistency, 18 to 20 minutes. Return the shanks to the liquid, cover to keep warm and set aside.

braised lamb shanks

6 lamb shanks, each 12 to 14 oz

Sea salt and cracked black pepper to taste

4 Tbsp extra-virgin olive oil

1 large onion, cut into ½-inch pieces

1 large carrot, cut into ½-inch pieces

2 stalks celery, cut into ½-inch pieces

2 cloves garlic, whole

2 Tbsp tomato paste

2 cups white wine

2 bay leaves

Large sprig of rosemary

5 cups Veal Stock (page 220) or chicken stock

As you can see, I like slow-cooked meats. I bet you will too. Cooking everything together in one pot concentrates the flavours. For this dish, use local lamb if it's available. We like the hind shanks, as they tend to be a little bit meatier than the front ones. You can prepare this dish several days in advance. Like most braised dishes, it tastes better with each passing day.

CARROT PURÉE Place the carrots in a saucepan, just cover with water and bring to a boil on high heat. Turn down the heat, cover the pot and cook for 10 minutes, or until the carrots are softened and tender when pierced with a fork. Drain the carrots, transfer them to a food processor and add the remaining ingredients. Purée at high speed until smooth. Check the seasoning. Return the carrot mixture to the pot, set aside in a warm place and reheat on low when needed.

TO SERVE Return the lamb shanks to medium-low heat and bring them to a simmer. Place a large spoonful of carrot in the middle of each plate, top with a lamb shank and spoon some braising liquid over top.

carrot purée

3 lb large carrots, peeled and sliced

½ tsp curry powder (we use a mild Madras)

½ cup whipping cream

¼ cup salted butter

1 Tbsp honey

Pinch of sea salt

vanilla doughnuts with earl grey tea ice cream

MILK CHOCOLATE AND EARL GREY TEA ICE CREAM Combine the cream, milk, Earl Grey tea and vanilla in a medium saucepan and bring to a boil on medium-high heat. Remove from the heat, cover tightly with a lid and let infuse for 10 minutes. Strain the mixture through a fine-mesh sieve into a clean saucepan. Squeeze out any excess liquid from the tea leaves and vanilla bean, then discard them. Set aside the infused milk mixture.

Have ready a stainless steel bowl that fits over a medium saucepan. Fill the pot ¼ full with water and bring to a simmer on medium-high heat. Place the chocolate in the bowl and set it over the water, stirring constantly with a rubber spatula until the chocolate has melted. Remove from the heat and set aside in a warm place.

Fill a large bowl with ice. Return the infused cream to medium-high heat and bring just to a boil.

In a large bowl, whisk together the egg yolks with the sugar until light and creamy. Gently pour the boiled cream over the yolks and sugar, whisking constantly, then return the entire mixture to the pot. Cook on medium heat, stirring constantly with a wooden spoon, until the mixture thickens enough to coat the back of the spoon. Remove from the heat. While still warm, strain the cream mixture through a fine-mesh sieve into the melted chocolate. Stir thoroughly to ensure all of the chocolate is melted. Set the bowl with the chocolate cream mixture over the bowl of ice and refrigerate for at least 4 hours, or overnight.

Once chilled, scrape the ice cream base into an ice cream maker and churn according to the manufacturer's instructions. This will keep in the freezer for up to 1 week.

milk chocolate and earl grey tea ice cream

2 cups whipping cream

¾ cup whole milk

2 Tbsp loose Earl Grey tea leaves

½ vanilla bean, split lengthwise and seeds scraped

4 oz milk chocolate (Valrhona or Lindt are good choices)

8 egg yolks

½ cup + 1 Tbsp granulated sugar

This classic Araxi dessert involves several steps, but the combination of Earl Grey and milk chocolate ice cream with warm sugary doughnuts is not to be missed. Shape these any way you like.

SPICE-INFUSED SUGAR Combine all of the ingredients in a bowl and mix thoroughly. This will keep in an airtight container at room temperature for up to 1 month.

VANILLA DOUGHNUTS Melt the butter with the water in a small pot on low heat. Allow this mixture to cool to lukewarm.

In the bowl of a stand mixer, stir together the warm milk and yeast. Set aside to bloom for 5 minutes. Mix the vanilla bean seeds into the sugar.

In a medium bowl, combine the vanilla sugar, flour, cinnamon, cardamom, pepper, vanilla, orange zest and salt.

Add the eggs to the milk and yeast mixture and fit the stand mixer with the paddle attachment. With the motor running at low speed, add ½ of the water-butter mixture to the egg mixture. Add ½ of the dry mixture and blend, then scrape down the sides of the bowl. Add the remaining wet ingredients and mix well, then add the remaining dry mixture. Mix until the dough has come together and is soft and sticky, about 3 minutes.

Lightly dust a clean work surface with flour and lightly grease a large bowl with oil. Turn the dough out onto the floured surface and knead gently by hand for 3 to 4 minutes. Shape the dough into a ball and place it in the bowl, cover with plastic wrap and refrigerate for 2 hours to let it proof.

Have ready a 3-inch round cookie cutter. Turn the dough out onto the lightly floured surface. Using a rolling pin, roll the dough into a rough circle about ½ inch thick. Cut out as many rounds as possible from the dough. (You can re-roll the scraps of dough and cut a few more.) Place the rounds on a plate and refrigerate, covered with a damp cloth, while you heat the oil for deep-frying.

continued overleaf

spice-infused sugar
1 cup granulated sugar
1 tsp ground cinnamon
¼ tsp ground nutmeg
¼ ground allspice
Seeds from 1 vanilla bean
Pinch of cayenne pepper

vanilla doughnuts
¼ cup unsalted butter, softened
1 cup water
2 Tbsp whole milk, warmed
2 Tbsp fresh yeast (or ¾ Tbsp dried yeast)
Seeds from 1 vanilla bean (reserve the pod to place in sugar for future use)
½ cup granulated sugar
5 cups all-purpose flour
¼ tsp ground cinnamon
Pinch of ground cardamom
Pinch of ground black pepper
Zest of 1 orange
2 tsp salt
2 large eggs
6 cups vegetable oil for deep-frying

Line a plate with paper towels. In a deep fryer, wok or deep-sided saucepan, heat the vegetable oil to 325°F. Check the temperature of the oil using a deep-fat thermometer. Once the oil is hot enough, add the doughnuts in batches of 5 or 6 and cook for about 2 minutes. Using a slotted spoon, carefully flip the doughnuts and cook the other side for a further 2 minutes. Transfer the cooked doughnuts to the lined plate to drain. Quickly cook the remaining doughnuts.

Place the spice-infused sugar in a small shallow bowl. While the cooked doughnuts are still warm, toss them in the bowl, coating them with generous amounts of the spiced sugar.

TO SERVE Scoop the Earl Grey ice cream into individual bowls. Garnish each serving with 3 doughnuts and serve immediately while the doughnuts are still warm.

maple sugar crème brûlées with shortbread

MAPLE SUGAR CRÈME BRÛLÉES Preheat the oven to 300°F. Arrange eight 4 oz ramekins in a deep baking dish.

Combine the cream, milk and vanilla in a medium saucepan and bring to a boil on medium-high heat. Remove from the heat.

In a large stainless steel bowl, whisk together the egg yolks, whole eggs, sugar and maple syrup until just combined. Do not overmix them. Gently pour a little bit of the scalded cream over the egg mixture, whisking constantly. Keep pouring small amounts of the cream over the egg mixture, whisking constantly, until all of the cream has been incorporated. Strain the mixture through a fine-mesh sieve into a clean bowl. Discard the solids. Pour the strained custard into the prepared ramekins, leaving at least ¼ inch free at the rim.

Have ready a large kettle of boiling water. Cover the baking dish containing the ramekins with aluminum foil, leaving one corner open. Pour the boiling water into the baking dish until it reaches ¾ of the way up the side of the ramekins. Seal the edge of the aluminum foil so the ramekins are fully enclosed and bake for 15 minutes. Carefully rotate the tray and bake for another 5 minutes. To check for doneness, gently shake the pan. The brûlées should jiggle slightly in the centre like Jell-O, but not be liquid. If they are still a bit liquid, turn off the oven, cover the baking dish with the aluminum foil and let the brûlées sit in the oven for about 5 minutes (keep an eye on them). The residual heat will continue to cook the brûlées.

When the brûlées are cooked, remove them from the oven, discard the foil and lift the ramekins out of the baking dish. Set the ramekins on a baking sheet and refrigerate them overnight.

maple sugar crème brûlées

2 cups whipping cream

1 cup whole milk

1 vanilla bean, split lengthwise and seeds scraped

6 egg yolks

2 whole eggs

½ cup granulated sugar

2 Tbsp maple syrup

2 Tbsp maple sugar, to serve

Nothing tastes better than maple syrup or sugar, and this dessert showcases that sweet flavour. Make these brûlées the day before you plan to serve them so they have plenty of time to set up. To caramelize the tops, we use a food-grade blowtorch, but if you don't have one you can use the broiler of your oven for similar results.

SHORTBREAD Preheat the oven to 325°F. In a small stand mixer fitted with the paddle attachment, cream the butter, ½ cup of the sugar, and the vanilla seeds at low speed until just soft, about 2 minutes.

Sift the flour, cornstarch and salt into a bowl, then add these dry ingredients to the butter mixture. Process at low speed until just combined. Do not overmix.

Lightly grease an 8½ × 11-inch baking tray with butter (or spray it with nonstick spray) and line it with parchment paper. Using a spatula, spread the shortbread dough evenly across the tray and bake for 20 minutes. Rotate the tray and bake for a further 20 minutes until the top of the shortbread is a nice golden brown.

Transfer the baking tray to a wire rack and sprinkle the warm shortbread evenly with the remaining sugar. While the shortbread is still warm on the baking tray, use a serrated knife to cut it into 24 evenly sized pieces. Allow to cool fully before removing the shortbread from the tray.

TO SERVE Remove the crème brûlées from the fridge and set them on a clean, uncluttered counter. Sprinkle the maple sugar evenly over the top of each one. Using a food-grade blowtorch, gently heat the maple sugar on each crème brûlée until it starts to caramelize and become golden brown. Place each ramekin on an individual plate and garnish with 3 pieces of shortbread.

shortbread

1½ cups + 1 Tbsp unsalted butter, very soft

1 cup granulated sugar, divided

Seeds from 1 vanilla bean

3 cups all-purpose flour

2 Tbsp cornstarch

½ tsp salt

apple &
almond tart
with whipped
sour cream

PÂTE BRISÉE Place the sifted flour, sugar, salt and vanilla seeds in a large bowl. Using the largest holes of a box grater, grate the cold butter into the bowl. (This little trick lets you get the butter in uniformly small pieces without warming it.) Gently disperse the butter pieces, breaking apart any of the larger pieces with your fingertips.

Have ready a large piece of plastic wrap. Make a "well" in the centre of the flour mixture and pour in all of the cold water. Using a pastry cutter, quickly work the water into the flour-butter mixture. Press the dough together using the backs of your knuckles to create a shaggy but cohesive mass. It will not look uniform—there will still be streaks of butter in the dough—but it should stay together. Form the dough into a rough flat disk, working it as little as possible, and wrap it in the plastic wrap. Refrigerate the dough until well chilled, at least 2 hours.

Using as little flour as possible, roll the dough out to a circle 14 inches in diameter and about ¼ inch thick. Try to roll the dough as round and as evenly as possible. Transfer the rolled dough to a baking tray, cover with plastic wrap or parchment paper and refrigerate for 20 minutes before transferring it to the tart ring.

Using either a fork or a dough docker, prick the pastry evenly. Gently slide both hands under the pastry and transfer it to the tart ring. Allow any excess dough to hang loosely over the sides as you use your fingers to work the dough into the bottom of the tart ring, being careful not to tear or overly stretch the dough. Lift up the edge of the dough as you press it into the bottom of the tart ring.

pâte brisée

2½ cups sifted all-purpose flour

1 tsp granulated sugar

Pinch of salt

Seeds from ½ vanilla bean

¾ cup + 1 Tbsp unsalted butter, cold

½ cup ice-cold water

apple filling

1 lemon, cut in half

15 medium-size crisp, sweet apples such as Pink Lady

1 cup granulated sugar

1 cinnamon stick, 4 inches long

½ vanilla bean, split lengthwise and seeds scraped

¼ cup good-quality honey (we like Golden Cariboo from Lillooet)

Not all apples make good tart fillings. We like Pink Lady or Crisp Pink or Granny Smith because they maintain their shape and structure when heated and aren't too mushy when cooked. Sour cream is a great foil for the sweetness of the apples and the toasted almonds, and is good with fresh berries.

To make this tart, use a 10-inch tart ring, straight-sided or fluted, about an inch and a half tall. You will also need a box grater with large holes to grate the butter. We refrigerate the dough after each step to keep the butter in it cold, which helps ensure that it will be flaky when cooked. Note that the sour cream needs to sit overnight before being used.

Loosely crimp the edge of the dough around the top where it will eventually be trimmed off after baking, leaving the extra dough attached. Refrigerate the dough in the tart ring for at least 30 minutes before blind baking.

Preheat the oven to 375°F. To blind bake the pastry, line it with aluminum foil. Fill it with pie weights or baking beans and bake for 20 minutes, until the edges are golden brown. Gently remove the pie weights and foil and return the pastry to the oven for 8 to 10 minutes, or until it is completely golden brown. Remove from the oven and set aside to cool in the tart ring on a wire rack while you prepare the apple filling and almond-streusel topping.

APPLE FILLING Squeeze the juice from the lemon into a large bowl and discard the peels. Peel and core the apples, then slice them thinly and toss these pieces in the lemon juice.

In a saucepan large enough to hold all of the apples, combine the sugar with enough water to just moisten (¼ cup or less). Cook over high heat (do not stir or the sugar may crystallize) until the sugar caramelizes to a dark golden. You can swirl the pan around to ensure even browning. Stir in the apples immediately along with the cinnamon and vanilla. Cook over high heat, stirring constantly until the apples are slightly translucent and slightly golden. Add the honey and continue to cook over high heat until almost all the liquid has evaporated, 5 to 10 minutes.

Transfer the cooked apples to a perforated pan or metal steamer set over a baking tray in the sink and let the apples cool at room temperature while any excess liquid drips out. Remove and discard the cinnamon stick. Meanwhile, prepare the topping and the sour cream. *continued overleaf*

almond-streusel topping

½ cup sifted all-purpose flour

½ cup granulated sugar

¼ cup ground almonds

¼ cup sliced almonds

½ cup unsalted butter, cold, cut in 1-inch cubes

Small pinch of sea salt

whipped sour cream

1 cup full-fat sour cream, wrapped in cheesecloth and hung overnight to remove excess liquid

1 Tbsp granulated sugar

1 cup whipping cream

ALMOND-STREUSEL TOPPING Combine all the ingredients in a medium bowl and work them together with your fingertips until the topping has the consistency of small peas. Spread the mixture on a baking tray and refrigerate until needed.

To assemble: Preheat the oven to 325°F. Arrange the cooked apples in the tart shell, pressing the slices in firmly. Sprinkle the almond-streusel topping over the apples and bake for about 15 minutes, until the streusel is golden brown. Remove from the oven and allow the tart to cool for at least 20 minutes before slicing.

WHIPPED SOUR CREAM Just before serving the tart, whisk together the sour cream with the sugar in a large bowl.

In a stand mixer fitted with the whisk attachment, whip the whipping cream at high speed until it forms firm peaks, 3 to 5 minutes. Using a spatula, gently fold the whipped cream into the sour cream mixture until well combined.

TO SERVE Place a slice of the apple tart on each plate and garnish with a large spoonful of whipped sour cream. Serve immediately.

| # sour cream coffee cake with poached pears

POACHED PEARS Place the sugar in a saucepan on high heat and cook, swirling the pan but not stirring, until it becomes a deep golden brown. Carefully pour in the white wine and water and continue cooking, stirring gently until the caramelized sugar has dissolved completely. Stir in the brandy, vanilla pods and peppercorns and bring to a boil, then turn down the heat to low.

Cut a circle of parchment paper the diameter of the pot containing the poaching liquid. Peel the pears, discarding their skins. Using a melon baller, scoop out the core and seeds through the bottom of each pear and discard. Cut the pears in half lengthwise and place them in the poaching liquid. Cover the pears with the parchment paper and simmer until just tender, 20 to 25 minutes. Remove from the heat.

While the pears are still warm, transfer the pears and the poaching liquid to an airtight container and allow to cool to room temperature with the lid off. Once cool, seal the lid and refrigerate for at least 6 hours or (best) overnight, until completely cool and the pears are infused with the flavour of the poaching liquid.

SOUR CREAM COFFEE CAKE Preheat the oven to 350°F. Grease a 5½ × 9½ × 3-inch loaf pan with the 1 Tbsp of butter and dust with the 2 Tbsp of flour. Set aside.

In a small bowl, combine the eggs, sour cream and vanilla seeds. Using a fork, whisk together until fully combined. Set aside.

In a second small bowl, sift together the 1¼ cups of flour, baking soda, baking powder and salt. Set aside.

poached pears

1 cup + 2 Tbsp granulated sugar

2 cups white wine

1 cup water

¼ cup brandy

2 vanilla beans, split lengthwise to expose the seeds

1 tsp black peppercorns

4 medium Anjou or Bartlett pears, firm and underripe

sour cream coffee cake

½ cup unsalted butter, very soft, + 1 Tbsp for greasing the pan

1¼ cups all-purpose flour + 2 Tbsp for dusting the pan

2 large eggs

1 cup full-fat sour cream

Seeds from 1 vanilla bean

2 tsp baking soda

2 tsp baking powder

⅛ tsp salt

1 cup granulated sugar

Poached pears are great at any time, on their own or used in recipes like this one. Served with freshly brewed tea or coffee, this comforting recipe is perfect for a rainy afternoon or a Sunday dinner. It is best served warm from the oven on the day it is made, with a dollop of whipped salted butter. If necessary, you can prepare this cake a day ahead, allow it to cool and then wrap it in plastic wrap and store at cool room temperature overnight. Before serving, preheat the oven to 275°F, remove the plastic wrap and wrap the cake in aluminum foil instead, then warm it for about 15 minutes until ready to serve.

Using a stand mixer fitted with the paddle attachment, cream together the ½ cup butter and the sugar at medium speed until light and fluffy, 3 to 5 minutes. Scrape down the sides of the bowl. Add the egg mixture all at once and mix at medium-low speed until just combined, about 2 minutes. Scrape down the sides of the bowl. Sift the dry ingredients, add to the bowl in one batch and mix at low speed until just combined, 1 minute. Do not overmix.

Using a rubber spatula, scrape the cake batter into the loaf pan and spread the top of the cake smooth. Bake for 20 minutes, then rotate the pan 90 degrees and bake for another 20 to 25 minutes, or until the tip of a clean, dry knife inserted in the centre comes out clean. Let the cake rest in the pan for 10 minutes, then remove from pan and transfer to a wire rack to cool for 30 minutes.

TO SERVE Remove the poached pears from the fridge and allow them to warm to room temperature. Slice the warm cake into 8 generous slices, each about 1 inch thick, and arrange on a serving platter. Cut the poached pear halves in half lengthwise and arrange them around the cake.

DARK CHOCOLATE
MOUSSE COUPES
page 216

TRIPLE CHOCOLATE
COOKIES
page 92

dark chocolate mousse coupes

DARK CHOCOLATE MOUSSE LAYER Have ready 6 glass dessert coupes or bowls, each 4 to 6 oz, and a stainless steel bowl that fits over a medium saucepan. Fill the pot ¼ full with water and bring to a simmer on high heat. Place the dark chocolate in the bowl and set it over the water, stirring with a rubber spatula until it has melted. Leave the pot on the heat, but set the bowl of melted chocolate in a warm place.

In a medium bowl, combine ½ cup of the whipping cream with the egg yolks and sugar and whisk until creamy. Set this bowl over the pot of simmering water (be sure that it is not boiling) and whisk until light and fluffy, 4 to 5 minutes. Using a spatula, fold the egg mixture into the melted chocolate and allow to cool to room temperature.

Place the remaining whipping cream in the bowl of a stand mixer fitted with the whisk attachment and beat at high speed until it forms firm peaks, about 3 to 4 minutes. Fold ⅓ of the whipped cream into the chocolate mixture, ensuring it is fully incorporated. Fold in the remaining cream and transfer the mixture to a piping bag fitted with a star tip. Immediately pipe the mousse into 6 glass coupes or small bowls and refrigerate, uncovered, until firm and well chilled, 2 to 3 hours.

dark chocolate mousse layer

7 oz dark chocolate (64% cocoa)

3 cups whipping cream

4 large egg yolks

3 Tbsp granulated sugar

2 cups unsweetened whipped cream, for garnish

1 oz chunk bittersweet chocolate, for garnish

This recipe is pretty chocolatey, but you can add fresh berries in between layers or as a garnish to balance it out. Toasted nuts are also always a welcome accompaniment to chocolate. You can make these coupes several days before you plan to serve them.

CHOCOLATE GLAZE Have ready a stainless steel bowl that fits over a medium saucepan. Fill the saucepan ¼ full with water and bring to a simmer on low heat. Place the dark chocolate and butter in the bowl and set it over the water, stirring with a rubber spatula until they melt together. Whisk in the simple syrup, glucose (or corn syrup) and rum then the cocoa powder and stir until completely smooth and glossy. Remove from the heat and let stand in a cool place for 10 to 15 minutes until the mixture reaches room temperature.

Whisk the glaze again to make it smooth and glossy and pour it in a thin layer over the prepared mousse coupes. Immediately return the mousses to the fridge for 15 minutes.

TO SERVE Garnish each of the mousses with enough whipped cream to reach the top of the coupe. Level the tops with a knife or a pastry scraper. Using a fine grater or a microplane, shave bits of bittersweet chocolate over each plate and serve.

chocolate glaze

5 oz dark chocolate (65 to 70% cocoa), roughly chopped

2 Tbsp unsalted butter, softened

½ cup Simple Syrup (page 219)

¼ cup glucose or clear corn syrup

2 tsp dark rum

1 Tbsp cocoa powder, sifted

basics

simple syrup

2 cups water
2 cups granulated sugar

Place the water and sugar in a small sauce-pan and whisk to combine. Cook on medium heat until the mixture comes to a boil and the sugar is dissolved. Remove from the heat and refrigerate for 45 minutes, until chilled. This will keep refrigerated in an airtight container for up to 2 weeks.

yuzu mayonnaise

2 egg yolks
¼ cup yuzu juice (available at Japanese grocers)
1 Tbsp Dijon mustard
2 cups grapeseed oil
Sea salt and ground white pepper to taste

In a blender, combine the egg yolks, yuzu juice and Dijon mustard at low speed until emulsified. With the motor running, slowly add the grapeseed oil in a thin stream until the mayonnaise becomes thick. Season with salt and white pepper, cover and refrigerate until chilled, about 1 hour. This will keep refrigerated in an airtight container for up to 3 days.

sesame-soy vinaigrette

4¼ oz fresh horseradish, washed and thinly sliced (½ cup)
1 cup soy sauce
¼ cup brown sugar, packed
8 green onions, green and white parts, minced
4 red jalapeño peppers, with seeds, minced
1 cup red wine vinegar
½ cup mirin
1½ cups grapeseed oil
½ cup sesame oil
Sea salt and ground black pepper to taste
24 drops Tabasco sauce

Combine the horseradish, soy sauce, sugar, green onions and jalapeños in a medium saucepan and bring to a boil over medium-high heat. Immediately turn down the heat to a simmer and cook until the liquid is reduced to 1 cup, 8 to 10 minutes.

Strain the liquid through a fine-mesh sieve into a clean bowl. Discard the solids. Pour in the red wine vinegar, mirin, and grapeseed and sesame oils. Season with salt and pepper, then stir in the Tabasco until well combined. This will keep refrigerated in an airtight container for up to 7 days.

vegetable nage

8 cloves garlic

8 shallots, sliced

5 carrots, sliced

4 stalks celery, sliced

2 onions, thinly siced

1 fennel bulb, thinly sliced

4 star anise

3 bay leaves

8 coriander seeds

8½ cups water

1 cup white wine

Have ready a large roasting pan full of ice. In a large stockpot, combine the vegetables, star anise, bay leaves and coriander seeds with the water and bring to a boil on high heat. Turn down the heat to low and simmer, uncovered, for 10 minutes. Remove from the heat and stir in the wine. Place the stockpot over the ice for 20 minutes and let cool. Strain the nage through a fine-mesh sieve and discard the solids. This will keep refrigerated in an airtight container for up to 7 days or frozen for up to 3 months.

veal stock

10 lb meaty veal bones (such as knuckles, skin and neck)

2 pig's feet

¼ cup grapeseed oil

2 onions, chopped

3 cloves garlic

3 large carrots, chopped

4 stalks celery, chopped

3 cups red wine

16 to 20 cups cold water

2 cups canned tomatoes, with their juice

½ cup tomato paste

10 black peppercorns

1 bay leaf

2 sprigs fresh parsley

Preheat the oven to 375°F. Place the veal bones and pig's feet in a deep roasting pan and roast for 40 to 45 minutes. Turn the bones and roast them for another 45 minutes to 1 hour, or until they are deep brown and the oils are cooked out. Transfer the bones and pig's feet to a large stockpot, pouring off and discarding any fat.

Heat the grapeseed oil in a large saucepan on medium-high heat. Add the onions, garlic, carrots and celery and cook until golden and caramelized, 10 to 12 minutes. Pour in the red wine and cook for 10 to 12 minutes, or until the wine has reduced almost completely. Stir in the remaining ingredients, except for the cold water, and cook for 6 to 8 minutes to concentrate the flavours. *continued opposite*

Add the vegetable mixture to the roasted bones, just cover with cold water and bring to a boil over high heat. Turn down the heat to medium and simmer, uncovered, skimming the surface frequently with a slotted spoon to remove any fat and foam, for 6 to 8 hours to retrieve all of the flavours. It should be deep brown in colour, but tasting is really the best way to tell when this is ready. Taste it regularly after the 6-hour point.

Set a fine-mesh sieve or a colander lined with cheesecloth over a clean bowl and strain the stock through it. Discard any solids. This will keep refrigerated in airtight container or resealable plastic bags for up to 10 days, or frozen in ice cube trays and then stored in resealable plastic bags for up to 3 months.

MAKES 2½ CUPS
Nora peppers are dried Spanish peppers that are readily available at European grocers, like Bosa Foods in Vancouver, or online.

romesco sauce

5 large tomatoes, cores removed and flesh cut in half (vine-ripened are good for this; about the size of a billiard ball)

1 head garlic, cut in half, skins on

2 medium nora peppers, soaked and drained, or 1 large bell pepper, cut in half and seeds removed

1 small chili pepper, cut in half and seeds removed (optional)

⅓ cup blanched whole almonds

1 large slice day-old crusty bread, cut into quarters

1 cup good-quality extra-virgin Spanish olive oil

¼ cup sherry vinegar

1 tsp sweet paprika

Preheat the oven to 375°F. Place the tomatoes, garlic, nora (or bell) peppers, chili pepper (if using), almonds and bread in a baking dish. Drizzle with ¼ cup of the olive oil, and bake for 15 to 20 minutes until the tomatoes soften, the garlic, bread and almonds are golden and the garlic is soft. Remove from the oven and set aside until cool enough to handle.

Squeeze the garlic cloves from their skins and discard the skins. Transfer the garlic and the entire contents of the baking dish to a blender or food processor. Add the remaining olive oil, the vinegar and paprika and season with sea salt. Blend at high speed until the sauce is thick and smooth. This will keep refrigerated in an airtight container for 2 to 3 days.

METRIC CONVERSION TABLE

volume

IMPERIAL	METRIC
⅛ tsp	0.5 mL
¼ tsp	1 mL
½ tsp	2.5 mL
¾ tsp	4 mL
1 tsp	5 mL
½ Tbsp	8 mL
1 Tbsp	15 mL
1½ Tbsp	23 mL
2 Tbsp	30 mL
¼ cup	60 mL
⅓ cup	80 mL
½ cup	125 mL
⅔ cup	165 mL
¾ cup	185 mL
1 cup	250 mL
1¼ cups	310 mL
1⅓ cups	330 mL
1½ cups	375 mL
1⅔ cups	415 mL
1¾ cups	435 mL
2 cups	500 mL
2¼ cups	560 mL
2⅓ cups	580 mL
2½ cups	625 mL
2¾ cups	690 mL
3 cups	750 mL
4 cups / 1 qt	1 L
5 cups	1.25 L
6 cups	1.5 L
7 cups	1.75 L
8 cups	2 L

liquid measures
(for alcohol)

IMPERIAL	METRIC
1 fl oz	30 mL
2 fl oz	60 mL
3 fl oz	90 mL
4 fl oz	120 mL

weight

IMPERIAL	METRIC
½ oz	15 g
1 oz	30 g
2 oz	60 g
3 oz	85 g
4 oz (¼ lb)	115 g
5 oz	140 g
6 oz	170 g
7 oz	200 g
8 oz (½ lb)	225 g
9 oz	255 g
10 oz	285 g
11 oz	310 g
12 oz (¾ lb)	340 g
13 oz	370 g
14 oz	400 g
15 oz	425 g
16 oz (1 lb)	450 g
1¼ lb	570 g
1½ lb	670 g
2 lb	900 g
3 lb	1.4 kg
4 lb	1.8 kg
5 lb	2.3 kg
6 lb	2.7 kg

temperature

IMPERIAL	METRIC
140°F	60°C
150°F	66°C
155°F	68°C
160°F	71°C
165°F	74°C
170°F	77°C
175°F	80°C
180°F	82°C
190°F	88°C
200°F	93°C
240°F	116°C
250°F	121°C
300°F	149°C
325°F	163°C
350°F	177°C
360°F	182°C
375°F	191°C

oven temperature

IMPERIAL	METRIC
200°F	95°C
250°F	120°C
275°F	135°C
300°F	150°C
325°F	160°C
350°F	180°C
375°F	190°C
400°F	200°C
425°F	220°C
450°F	230°C

linear

IMPERIAL	METRIC
⅛ inch	3 mm
¼ inch	6 mm
½ inch	12 mm
¾ inch	2 cm
1 inch	2.5 cm
1¼ inches	3 cm
1½ inches	3.5 cm
1¾ inches	4.5 cm
2 inches	5 cm
2½ inches	6.5 cm
3 inches	7.5 cm
4 inches	10 cm
5 inches	12.5 cm
6 inches	15 cm
7 inches	18 cm
10 inches	25 cm
12 inches (1 foot)	30 cm
13 inches	33 cm
16 inches	41 cm
18 inches	46 cm
24 inches (2 feet)	60 cm
28 inches	70 cm
30 inches	75 cm

ACKNOWLEDGEMENTS

I WOULD LIKE TO THANK the many people who had a hand in making this, our second cookbook, possible. To start, the Aquilini family for their faith and belief in us at Toptable Restaurant Group and their vision for the future. A huge debt of gratitude to Michael Doyle at Toptable Group and Canucks Sports & Entertainment, who got this book started, for all his support.

A very special thank-you for all their wisdom, passion and kindness to my mentor Jack Evrensel and his wife, Araxi, who created the restaurant that we love so much.

To my partner at Araxi, restaurant director Neil Henderson, and to pastry chef Aaron Heath, thank you for so many shared memories and restaurant services. And thanks, Aaron, for your contributions to the dessert recipes for this cookbook and our first one.

Further thanks to my Chef Squad extraordinaire, past and present: Jeff Park, Mark McLoughlin, Andreas Wechselberger, Yoann Therer, Yutaka Shishido, Frederic Czapek and Jorge Muñoz Santos, and the whole brigade, many of whom have helped develop recipes in this book.

The service team at Araxi who make so many things possible: Samantha Rahn, Darin Newton, Rene Wuethrich, Pat Allan, Tova Johnson, Jason Kawaguchi, and notably, Jason Redmond, who contributed all of the cocktail recipes for this book.

The Toptable head office team who keep us in line and on the course: Lynn Gervais, April Penney, Alexander Wilde and Min Jee.

We were thrilled to be working again with Lucy Kenward and Chris Labonté on this project, and a very special thank-you also to Jessica Sullivan and all the folks at Figure 1 for their creative insight and incredible patience.

A big shout-out to Andrew Morrison for all the nice stories and great afternoon chats that he turned into the brilliant text in this book. You can't go wrong with creative people.

To Alison Page and Issha Marie for their incredible photography, energy, passion and ability to see images before they happen and capture them. We had lots of fun at the farm, eh?

And a special thank-you to Janaki Larsen, for the beautiful ceramics used to plate the dishes; Union Wood Co. and North Arm Farm, for the background props; and the Atkinsons of Parched Penguin, for the stunning glassware used to photograph the cocktails.

In these pages we tried to feature as many as possible of the farmers, producers, fishermen and foragers that we work with. They, along with our loyal patrons and supporters, make everything we strive for possible.

And last but not least, thanks to my lovely wife, Tina, for all she has done for me personally and for supporting me professionally for the last twenty years, and our two wonderful and amazing children, Henry and Ruby.

PEAS OUT.

INDEX

Photos are referenced in *italics*.

"00" flour, 64, 76–77, 117

A

albacore tuna in olive oil, lemon & herbs, 157
albacore tuna "niçoise" salad sticks, *44*, 45
almond-streusel topping, 209–11
apple & almond tart with whipped sour cream,
    208–11, *210*
apple dressing & geoduck clams with shaved
    fennel, *160*, 161
araxi après fondue, *184*, 185
asparagus & peas with pork jowls, *79*, 80–81
assorted tomato salad & crispy squash blossoms,
    112–13, 114–15
avocado, barbecued, small shrimp in, *34*, 35

B

baby gem lettuce with dill dressing, *144*, 145
bacon, fresh, with carrots & mustard vinaigrette,
    194–95, *196*
beef cheeks, slow-cooked, in port wine, *197*,
    198–99
beef steak. *see* "stretch the steak" tartine with
    aged provolone
beef tenderloin, whole, grilled, with green tomato
    salsa, *126*, 127–29, *128–29*
beet salsa with sunshine coast sturgeon
    & caviar, *180*, 181
beets, roasted, with chickpea caponata
    & nasturtium pesto, *149*, 150–51
berry mignonette, *158*, 159
biscuit dough, sablé, 101
blackberries with warm chocolate tart,
    98–99
blue bird, 28

blueberries & mint with lavender meringues,
    88–89, *90–91*
braised lamb shanks with carrot purée, 200–201
bramble on, 111
bread. *see* sandwiches
brine, duck, 80, 186–87
broccoli with flaked lingcod "chowder," 70–71
brochettes, grilled wild scallop, with summer
    vegetables, *39*, 40–41
broth. *see* sauces, stocks and dressings
brussels sprouts, 146
burrata & confit heirloom tomatoes, 53
buttermilk panna cotta with strawberries, 93

C

cake, flourless chocolate, 94–95
cake, sour cream coffee, with poached pears,
    212–13
caponata, chickpea, *149*, 151
carrot & coriander soup, *147*, 148
carrot purée with braised lamb shanks, 200–201
carrots with fresh bacon & mustard vinaigrette,
    194–95, *196*
cauliflower tempura with seared wild scallops,
    171, 172–73
caviar, salmon, *50*, 51
caviar, sturgeon, *180*, 181
CHEESE
    aged provolone with "stretch the steak"
        tartine, *192*, 193
    araxi après fondue, *184*, 185
    buffalo mozzarella with peperonata, *54*, 55
    burrata & confit heirloom tomatoes, 53
    crispy squash blossoms & assorted tomato
        salad, *112–13*, 114–15
    fonduto with oysters baked in seaweed,
        174–75, 176

grilled cheese garnish with roasted roma
    tomato soup, 52
manchego cheese & grilled bread with
    romesco, 156
ricotta gnudi with peas & mint, *116*, 117
stinging nettle gnocchi & king crab, *63*, 64–65
cherry ice cream bars, 94–97, *96*
chicken, romy's, under the brick, 82–83
chickpea caponata with roasted beets &
    nasturtium pesto, *149*, 150–51
chili-yuzu marinade, 46
chilled oysters with three mignonettes, *158*, 159
chilled poached salmon with cucumber and
    yogurt, 60–61, *62*
chive and olive oil vinaigrette, 30
chocolate & orange marshmallow treats,
    100–103, *102*
chocolate cake, flourless, 94–95
chocolate cookies, triple, 92, *214–15*
chocolate mousse coupes, dark, *214–15*, 216–17
chocolate tart, warm, with blackberries, 98–99
chorizo-crusted lingcod with tomato fondue,
    67, 68–69
clams, geoduck, with shaved fennel & apple
    dressing, *160*, 161
COCKTAILS
    blue bird, 28
    bramble on, 111
    firecracker margarita, 143
    gin & tonic, 110
    harmonious shake, 140
    otro loco mas, 26
    peach sangria, 27
    sin city, 141
    truth & lies, 29
    up the creek, 142
coffee cake, sour cream, with poached pears,
    212–13
compote, blueberry, 88–89, 91
confit heirloom tomatoes & burrata, 53
cookies, triple chocolate, 92, *214–15*
coriander & carrot soup, 147, *148*
corn salsa, 168, *170*
crab, dungeness, in egg crepe with yuzu gel,
    36–37, *38*
crab, king & stinging nettle gnocchi, *63*, 64–65
crab cakes, dungeness, with corn salsa,
    168–69, *170*
crème brûlées, maple sugar, with shortbread,
    206–7

crepe, egg (tamago), 36
crispy oyster "po' boy" tacos & salsa verde,
    166–67
cucumber and yogurt with chilled poached
    salmon, 60–61, *62*
cucumber-basil mignonette, *158*, 159
curry dressing with roasted prawns, *56*, 57

D
dark chocolate mousse coupes, *214–15*, 216–17
dill dressing, 121, 145
doughnuts, vanilla, with earl grey tea ice cream,
    202–5, *204*
dressings. *see* sauces, stocks and dressings
duck breasts, seared, with fresh horseradish
    & sesame, 186–87, *188*
duck brine, 80, 186–87
duck egg pasta tortellini with duck confit filling,
    76–77, *78*
dungeness crab cakes with corn salsa,
    168–69, *170*
dungeness crab in egg crepe with yuzu gel,
    36–37, *38*

E
EGGS
    baby gem lettuce with dill dressing, *144*, 145
    duck egg pasta tortellini with duck confit
        filling, 76–77, *78*
    egg crepe (tamago), 36
    soft-boiled, with sautéed wild mushrooms,
        154, 155

F
fennel, shaved, with geoduck clams & apple
    dressing, *160*, 161
firecracker margarita, 143
FISH. *see also* seafood
    albacore tuna in olive oil, lemon & herbs, 157
    albacore tuna "niçoise" salad sticks, *44*, 45
    chilled poached salmon with cucumber and
        yogurt, 60–61, *62*
    chorizo-crusted lingcod with tomato fondue,
        67, 68–69
    flaked lingcod "chowder" with broccoli, 70–71
    hot-smoked chinook salmon & marinated
        watermelon, 47–49, *48*
    roasted sablefish tail on root vegetables,
        178–79
    sockeye salmon chirashi, *50*, 51

sunshine coast sturgeon & caviar with beet
   salsa, *180*, 181
whole wild salmon baked in a salt crust, *120,
   121*, *122–25*
wild salmon tartare with seaweed, 46
flaked lingcod "chowder" with broccoli, 70–71
flour, Italian "00," 64, 76–77, 117
flourless chocolate cake, 94–95
fondue, après, araxi, *184*, 185
fonduto with oysters baked in seaweed,
   174–75, 176
fresh bacon with carrots & mustard vinaigrette,
   194–95, *196*

G

geoduck clams with shaved fennel & apple
   dressing, *160*, 161
gin & tonic, 110
gnocchi, stinging nettle & king crab,
   63, 64–65
gnudi, ricotta, with peas & mint, *116*, 117
green tomato salsa, *126*, 127
grilled bread with romesco & manchego
   cheese, 156
grilled cheese garnish with roasted roma tomato
   soup, 52
grilled neon squid with salsify, 59
grilled octopus "jorge style," *162*, 164–65
grilled wild scallop brochettes with summer
   vegetables, *39*, 40–41

H

harmonious shake, 140
herb glaze, fresh, with spot prawn sashimi, 33
honey syrup, 26
hot-smoked chinook salmon & marinated
   watermelon, 47–49, *48*

I

I love brussels sprouts, 146
ice cream bars, cherry, 94–97, *96*
ice cream, milk chocolate & earl grey tea,
   202, *204*
ice cream, vanilla, 94
Italian "00" flour, 64, 76–77, 117

L

lamb meatballs, spiced, "bar oso," 86–87
lamb shanks, braised, with carrot purée,
   200–201

lavender meringues with blueberries & mint,
   88–89, 90–91
lavender-infused simple syrup, 29
lettuce, baby gem, with dill dressing, *144*, 145
lingcod, chorizo-crusted, with tomato fondue, *67*,
   68–69
lingcod, flaked, "chowder" with broccoli, 70–71

M

manchego cheese & grilled bread with
   romesco, 156
maple sugar crème brûlées with shortbread,
   206–7
mark's rabbit sausage, *189*, 190–91
mayonnaise, yuzu, 35, 37, 169, 219
meatballs, lamb, spiced, "bar oso," 86–87
meringues, lavender, with blueberries & mint,
   88–89, 90–91
mignonettes, with chilled oysters, *158*, 159
montadito, 156
mozzarella, buffalo, with peperonata, *54*, 55
mushroom velouté, wild, 153
mushrooms, wild, sautéed, with soft-boiled
   eggs, *154*, 155
mussel chowder, 70
mussel broth, 70
mustard vinaigrette, 195

N

nage, vegetable, 30, 59, 77, 80, 117, 220
nasturtium pesto, *149*, 150
neon squid, grilled, with salsify, 59

O

octopus, grilled, "jorge style," *162*, 164–65
olive oil and chive vinaigrette, 30
orange marshmallow & chocolate treats,
   100–103, *102*
orange-scented pastry cream, 134
otro loco mas, 26
oyster "po' boy" tacos, crispy & salsa verde,
   166–67
oysters, chilled, with three mignonettes, *158*, 159
oysters baked in seaweed with fonduto,
   174–75, 176

P

pan-fried potatoes, 165
panna cotta, buttermilk, with strawberries, 93
pasta dough, duck egg, 76

pastry cream, orange-scented, 134

pâte brisée, 208

pâte sucrée, 98, 134

peach purée, 168–69, *170*

peach sangria, 27

pears, poached, 212

peas & mint with ricotta gnudi, *116*, 117

peas & asparagus with pork jowls, *79*, 80–81

peperonata with buffalo mozzarella, *54*, 55

pesto, nasturtium, *149*, 150

poached pears with sour cream coffee cake,
    212–13

pomme purée, *197*, 199

pork belly. *see* fresh bacon with carrots
    & mustard vinaigrette

pork jowls with asparagus and peas, *79*, 80–81

POTATOES
    pan-fried, 165
    pomme purée, *197*, 199

prawn, spot, corn & herb risotto, 74–75

prawn, spot, sashimi with fresh herb glaze, 33

prawns, roasted, with curry dressing, *56*, 57

Q

quinoa & spring vegetable salad, 30–31

R

rabbit sausage, mark's, *189*, 190–91

raisin vinaigrette, *171*, 172–73

raspberry tartlets, *132–33*, 134–35

rice, sushi, *50*, 51

ricotta gnudi with peas & mint, *116*, 117

risotto, spot prawn, corn & herb, 74–75

roasted beets with chickpea caponata &
    nasturtium pesto, *149*, 150–51

roasted prawns with curry dressing, *56*, 57

roasted roma tomato soup with grilled cheese
    garnish, 52

roasted sablefish tail on root vegetables, 178–79

romesco sauce, *42*, 43, 156, 164–65,
    193, 221

romy's chicken under the brick, 82–83

root vegetables, roasted sablefish tail on, 178–79

rosemary-roasted shallots, 83

S

sablé biscuit dough, 101

sablefish tail, roasted, on root vegetables,
    178–79

sage-infused simple syrup, 111

SALAD. *see also* vegetables
    albacore tuna "niçoise" salad sticks, *44*, 45
    assorted tomato salad & crispy squash blos-
        soms, *112–13*, 114–15
    baby gem lettuce with dill dressing, *144*, 145
    geoduck clams with shaved fennel & apple
        dressing, *160*, 161
    quinoa & spring vegetable salad, 30–31
    seaweed with wild salmon tartare, 46

salmon, hot-smoked chinook & marinated
    watermelon, 47–49, *48*

salmon, poached, chilled, with cucumber and
    yogurt, 60–61, *62*

salmon, whole wild, baked in a salt crust, *120*,
    121, *122–25*

salmon chirashi, sockeye, *50*, 51

salmon tartare, wild, with seaweed, 46

SALSA. *see also* sauces, stocks and dressings
    beet, *180*, 181
    corn, 168, *170*
    green tomato, *126*, 127
    tarragon, 83
    verde, *44*, 45, 166

SANDWICHES
    grilled bread with romesco & manchego
        cheese, 156
    grilled cheese garnish with roasted roma
        tomato soup, 52
    "stretch the steak" tartine with aged provolone,
        192, 193

sashimi, spot prawn, with fresh herb glaze, 33

SAUCES, STOCKS AND DRESSINGS. *see also* salsa
    apple dressing, 161
    berry mignonette, *158*, 159
    chili-yuzu marinade, 46
    chocolate glaze, *214–15*, 217
    chocolate sauce, semisweet, 101–3, *102*
    cucumber-basil mignonette, *158*, 159
    curry dressing, *56*, 57
    dill dressing, 121, 145
    duck brine, 80, 186–87
    finishing glaze, 77, *78*
    herb glaze, fresh, 33
    mignonettes, *158*, 159
    mussel broth, 70
    mustard vinaigrette, 195
    nasturtium pesto, *149*, 150
    pastry cream, orange scented, 134
    peach purée, 168–69, *170*
    raisin vinaigrette, *171*, 172–73

romesco sauce, *42, 43*, 156, 164–65, 193,
 194, 221
sesame-soy vinaigrette, 59, 186–87, *188*, 219
sweet and sour plum mignonette, *158*, 159
tomato sauce, 86
veal stock, 198, 200, 220–21
vegetable nage, 30, 59, 77, 80, 117, 220
yuzu mayonnaise, 35, 37, 169, 219
SAUSAGE
 chorizo-crusted lingcod with tomato fondue,
  67, 68–69
 mark's rabbit sausage, *189*, 190–91
sautéed wild mushrooms with soft-boiled eggs,
 154, 155
scallop brochettes, wild, grilled, with summer
 vegetables, *39*, 40–41
scallop carpaccio with basil & helen's oil, *42, 43*
scallops, wild, seared, with cauliflower tempura,
 171, 172–73
scallops in the shell with sea urchin butter, 177
SEAFOOD
 chilled oysters with three mignonettes,
  158, 159
 crispy oyster "po' boy" tacos & salsa verde,
  166–67
 dungeness crab cakes with corn salsa,
  168–69, *170*
 dungeness crab in egg crepe with yuzu gel,
  36–37, *38*
 geoduck clams with shaved fennel & apple
  dressing, *160*, 161
 grilled neon squid with salsify, 59
 grilled octopus "jorge style," *162*, 164–65
 grilled wild scallop brochettes with summer
  vegetables, *39*, 40–41
 king crab & stinging nettle gnocchi, *63*, 64–65
 oysters baked in seaweed with fonduto,
  174–75, 176
 roasted prawns with curry dressing, *56*, 57
 scallop carpaccio with basil & helen's oil,
  42, 43
 scallops in the shell with sea urchin
  butter, 177
 seared wild scallops with cauliflower
  tempura, *171*, 172–73
 small shrimp in barbecued avocado, *34*, 35
 spot prawn, corn & herb risotto, 74–75
 spot prawn sashimi with fresh herb glaze, 33
seared duck breasts with fresh horseradish
 & sesame, 186–87, *188*

seared wild scallops with cauliflower tempura,
 171, 172–73
seaweed, oysters baked in, with fonduto,
 174–75, 176
seaweed with wild salmon tartare, 46
semisweet chocolate sauce, 101–3
sesame-soy vinaigrette, 59, 186–87, *188*, 219
shallots, rosemary-roasted, 83
shortbread with maple sugar crème brûlées,
 206–7
shrimp, small, in barbecued avocado, *34*, 35
SIMPLE SYRUP, 36, 93, 134, 143, 219
 lavender-infused, 29
 sage-infused, 111
sin city, 141
slow-cooked beef cheeks in port wine, *197*,
 198–99
small shrimp in barbecued avocado, *34*, 35
sockeye salmon chirashi, *50*, 51
SOUP
 carrot & coriander soup, 147, *148*
 flaked lingcod "chowder" with broccoli, 70–71
 roasted roma tomato soup with grilled cheese
  garnish, 52
 wild mushroom velouté, 153
sour cream coffee cake with poached pears,
 212–13
sour cream, whipped, 209–11
spiced lamb meatballs "bar oso," 86–87
spice-infused sugar, 203, *204*
spot prawn, corn & herb risotto, 74–75
spot prawn sashimi with fresh herb glaze, 33
squash blossoms, crispy & assorted tomato
 salad, *112–13*, 114–15
squid, neon, grilled, with salsify, 59
stinging nettle gnocchi & king crab, *63*, 64–65
stock. *see* sauces, stocks and dressings
strawberries with buttermilk panna cotta, 93
"stretch the steak" tartine with aged provolone,
 192, 193
streusel topping, almond, 209–11, *210*
sugar, spice-infused, 203, *204*
sunshine coast sturgeon & caviar with beet
 salsa, *180*, 181
sushi rice, *50*, 51
sweet and sour plum mignonette, *158*, 159
syrup, honey, 26
SYRUP, SIMPLE, 36, 93, 134, 143, 219
 lavender-infused, 29
 sage-infused, 111

T

tacos, crispy oyster "po' boy" & salsa verde, 166–67

tamago, 36

tarragon salsa, 83

tart, apple & almond, with whipped sour cream, 208–11, *210*

tart, warm chocolate, with blackberries, 98–99

tartine, "stretch the steak," with aged provolone, *192*, 193

tartlets, raspberry, *132–33*, 134–35

tea ice cream, earl grey, with vanilla doughnuts, 202–5, *204*

tempura, cauliflower, with seared wild scallops, *171*, 172–73

tomato fondue with chorizo-crusted lingcod, *67*, 68–69

tomato salad, assorted & crispy squash blossoms, *112–13*, 114–15

tomato salsa, green, *126*, 127

tomato sauce, 86

tomato soup, roasted roma, with grilled cheese garnish, 52

tomatoes, heirloom, confit & burrata, 53

tortellini, duck egg pasta, with duck confit filling, 76–77, *78*

triple chocolate cookies, 92

truth & lies, 29

tuna, albacore, in olive oil, lemon & herbs, 157

tuna, albacore, "niçoise" salad sticks, *44*, 45

U

up the creek, 142

V

vanilla doughnuts with earl grey tea ice cream, 202–5, *204*

vanilla ice cream, 94

veal stock, 198, 200, 220–21

vegetable nage, 30, 59, 77, 80, 117, 220

VEGETABLES. *see also* salad

asparagus and peas with pork jowls, *79*, 80–81

barbecued avocado, small shrimp in, *34*, 35

broccoli with flaked lingcod "chowder," 70–71

carrot purée with braised lamb shanks, 200–201

carrots with fresh bacon & mustard vinaigrette, 194–95, *196*

cauliflower tempura with seared wild scallops, *171*, 172–73

confit heirloom tomatoes & burrata, 53

cucumber and yogurt with chilled poached salmon, 60–61, *62*

I love brussels sprouts, 146

mushrooms, wild, sautéed, with soft-boiled eggs, *154*, 155

pan-fried potatoes, 165

peperonata with buffalo mozzarella, *54*, 55

pomme purée, *197*, 199

roasted beets with chickpea caponata & nasturtium pesto, *149*, 150–51

root vegetables, roasted sablefish tail on, 178–79

rosemary-roasted shallots, 83

salsify with grilled neon squid, 59

summer vegetables with grilled wild scallop brochettes, *39*, 40–41

tomato fondue with chorizo-crusted lingcod, *67*, 68–69

VINAIGRETTE

mustard, 195

olive oil and chive, 30

raisin, *171*, 172–73

sesame-soy, 59, 186–87, *188*, 219

W

warm chocolate tart with blackberries, 98–99

watermelon, marinated & hot-smoked chinook salmon, 47–49, *48*

whole grilled beef tenderloin with green tomato salsa, *126*, 127–29, *128–29*

whole wild salmon baked in a salt crust, *120*, 121, *122–25*

wild mushroom velouté, 153

wild salmon tartare with seaweed, 46

Y

yuzu gel, 36, *38*

yuzu mayonnaise, 35, 37, 169, 219

yuzu-chili marinade, 46